300 Ways To Make the BEST CHRISTMAS EVER!

300 WAYS To Make the BEST CHRISTMAS EVER!

Decorations, Carols,
Crafts & Recipes for Every
Kind of Christmas Tradition

Edited by Mimi Tribble

Sterling Publishing Co., Inc.
New York

Library of Congress Cataloging-in-Publication Data Available

2   4   6   8   10   9   7   5   3   1

Published by Sterling Publishing Co., Inc.
387 Park Avenue South, New York, NY 10016
This book is comprised of material from the following Sterling titles:
Christmas Naturals © 1991 by Altamont Press
A Crafter's Book of Santas © 1996 by Altamont Press
Complete Home Bartender's Guide © 2002 by Salvatore Calabrese
Decorate Your Home for Christmas © 1996 by Chapelle, Ltd.
Have a Very Merry Tole-Painted Christmas © 2002 by Chapelle Ltd.
The Holiday Wreath Book © 1992 by Altamont Press
Last-Minute Christmas Gifts © 1995 by Altamont Press
Making Great Gingerbread Houses © 1999 by Lark Books
Wreath Magic © 1994 by Altamont Press

© 2004 by Sterling Publishing Co., Inc.
Distributed in Canada by Sterling Publishing
c/o Canadian Manda Group, One Atlantic Avenue, Suite 105
Toronto, Ontario, Canada M6K 3E7
Distributed in Great Britain by Chrysalis Books Group PLC
The Chrysalis Building, Bramley Road, London W10 6SP, England
Distributed in Australia by Capricorn Link (Australia) Pty. Ltd.
P.O. Box 704, Windsor, NSW 2756, Australia

Designed by Liz Trovato
Printed in China

Sterling 1-4027-1685-0

INTRODUCTION

6

Chapter One

TRADITIONAL AMERICAN CHRISTMAS

9

Chapter Two

VICTORIAN CHRISTMAS

35

Chapter Three

COUNTRY CHRISTMAS

81

Chapter Four

SOUTHWESTERN CHRISTMAS

111

Chapter Five

TRADITIONAL INTERNATIONAL CHRISTMAS

139

Chapter Six

NOT-QUITE GROWN-UP CHRISTMAS

163

APPENDIX OF TECHNIQUES

185

INDEX

221

Introduction

Enormously popular and wonderfully sentimental, Christmas is a holiday beloved for its many, many fabulous religious and cultural traditions. Some of these traditions are unique to individual families, while others extend throughout a region. Unlike other holidays, Christmas does not honor a political figure or historical event unique to one country nor as a religious holiday is it a day or season of atonement and repentance; rather, Christmas is a time for celebration and enjoyment. These ideas of traditions, family, and culture are essential to this book. *300 Ways to Make the Best Christmas Ever!* highlights popular Christmas traditions from a variety of backgrounds and offers suggestions to incorporate these customs into your festivities.

In order to capture the multitude of ways of how Christmas is celebrated cross-culturally, each chapter of this book focuses on a particular angle from regions to historical eras to Christmas for the young and the young at heart. The chapters are filled with ideas, which vary widely from popular stories and carols to decorations and crafts to special feasts and foods.

For example, read to your family the quintessential American Christmas story: "A Visit from Saint Nicholas" or sing the beloved-Victorian carol, "Hark the Harold Angels Sing." Bring country-style into your celebration by creating a Snow-Covered Cottage, reminiscent of white Christmases and horse-driven sleighs. Let your life and style determine how you decorate your home: for example, for those with a Southwestern flair, you can celebrate Christmas with cowboy boots and chili pepper wreaths. And for the young at heart, you can create delightful Santa toys or tole-paint a sled.

Many of the suggestions in this book are deeply rooted in the rich history of the Christmas story and its evolution into perhaps the most popular holiday. While Christians have celebrated the birth of Jesus since 98 AD, it was not until 357 AD that the present-day form of Christmas took its shape. For many years, the Christian church was appalled at Saturnalia, the Roman celebration of their god, a week of festivities marked by massive orgies and other acts of heathenism. In order to discourage Christian participation in these activities, the Church proclaimed December 25th, the main day of Saturnalia, as the official birthday of Jesus, marked by a feast of remembrance. While the orgies were left to the Romans, other customs of Saturnalia carried over to the Christian celebration of Christmas and are reminiscent in many of today's traditions. They include decking the halls with greenery, decorating trees, stringing lights and candles, and exchanging gifts.

Christmas and its accompanying festivities bring families together not only to remember the birth of Jesus, but also to show gratitude and thanksgiving for each other.

As customs have evolved over time, families have adapted them and personalized them through their own use and through the culture of the region. Take for example, the figure of Santa Claus, a religious and cultural icon. Santa Claus is based on a 4th-Century AD Turkish Bishop, Nicholas, who loved children and used to throw gifts through the windows of poor children. The Roman Catholic Church proclaimed Nicholas the patron saint of children and honor him on December 6th. A tradition still celebrated throughout Europe, on December 6th, children leave their shoes out and they are filled with gifts from *der Weinachtsmann* in Germany, Father Christmas in England, and *Sinter Klaas* in Holland. The Saint Nicholas of Europe is often portrayed as a slender man, in long robes of gray and other muted shades. (Make your own old-world Wondrous Santa, instructions on pages 151-53)

The American version of Santa Claus leaves gifts for children who hang their stockings on Christmas Eve. While the Dutch brought Santa Claus across the ocean in the early 17th Century, the 19th Century popularized the story of Santa and the 20th Century commercialized the legend. In 1809, Washington Irving in the *History of New York*, retold the Dutch tale. Then in 1824, elaborating on Irving's tale, Clement Clarke Moore, in a "Visit from Saint Nicholas," immortalized Santa as an elf, hopping from chimney to chimney with eight reindeer, giving all the good little boys and girls presents for their goodness. In the 1860s, illustrator Thomas Nast gave the American Santa his trademark red suit. Beginning in 1931, Coca-Cola® advertisements gave Santa life as a human and not just an elf. (The Santa used in the Santa Wreath, page 23, is a wonderful example of a more human, less fantasy, Santa.) The legend of Santa was further detailed in 1939 by Montgomery Ward advertisements that introduced a ninth reindeer, Rudolph, whose red nose guides Santa on foggy nights.

To answer children's questions about Santa's home and his family, where the toys come from, and what the reindeer do the rest of the year, various cultures have created their own versions. The Finnish claim that the reindeer graze on Lapland's

Korvatunturi or "Ear Fell," while Santa, who lives nearby, listens to who has been good and bad. Americans still favor the legend of Santa and his diligent elves living and working at undisclosed North Pole workshop.

The various versions of Santa Claus exemplify the wide-reach of Christmas traditions, historically, globally, and individually. Every family has their own version of Santa, maybe it's with Dad's hair peeking through, or every year Santa leaves a special something.

But Santa Claus, with his various legends and descriptions, is just one instance of the wide-appeal of Christmas. For more examples, ideas, and ways to make the best

Christmas ever from an American angle, a Victorian perspective, with country style, an International flair, or with youthful sentiments, read on. The appendix offers tips and techniques for many of the projects presented in the book from making fabulous gingerbread houses to creating your own delightful wreaths to perfecting the art of tole-painting. The stories, carols, crafts, decorations, recipes and everything else in *300 Ways to Make the Best Christmas Ever!* will inspire you and teach you to build upon your own customs and celebrations to make a fun, festive, and very merry Christmas!

Chapter One

TRADITIONAL AMERICAN CHRISTMAS

• • • • • • • • • • • •

Filled with American influences on the Christmas holiday, this chapter celebrates the time-honored customs of an American Christmas and will inspire you to incorporate these traditional ideas into your Christmas festivities. You can create a memorable holiday that celebrates American customs in a variety of ways. You can embrace popular American culture from the classic carols "Away in a Manger" and "Up on the Housetop" to the beloved story "The Gift of the Magi" by the prolific American writer O. Henry to the American rendering of Santa Claus, round-faced and rosy-cheeked. Or you can decorate for Christmas using indigenous American materials with a Pine Wreath or Evergreen Swag. Create scenes of an American Christmas with Painted Egg Ornaments and a Classic Gingerbread House. Or simply sip a mug of Eggnog, a classic Christmas favorite, in front of an open fire. Whatever you fancy, you can adapt these ideas to your personal style and create your own unique American Christmas.

Away in a Manger

(1887)

1.

Away in a manger, no crib for a bed
The little Lord Jesus laid down his sweet head
The stars in the bright sky looked down where he lay
The little Lord Jesus asleep on the hay

2.

The cattle are lowing, the baby awakes
But little Lord Jesus no crying He makes
I love Thee Lord Jesus. Look down from the sky
And stay by my side until morning is nigh

3.

Be near me Lord Jesus, I ask Thee to stay
Close by me for ever and love me I pray
Bless all the dear children in Thy tender care
And fit us for heaven to live with Thee there

We Three Kings

1.

We three kings of orient are
Bearing gifts we traverse afar
Field and fountain, moor and
    mountain
Following yonder star
Star of wonder, star of night
Star of royal beauty bright
Westward leading, still proceeding
Guide us to Thy perfect light

2.

Born a King on Bethlehem's
    plain
Gold I bring to crown Him again
King forever, ceasing never
Over us all to reign

3.

Frankincense to offer have I
Incense owns a Deity nigh
Prayer and praising, all men raising
Worship Him, God most high

4.

Myrrh is mine, its bitter perfume
Breathes a life of gathering gloom
Sorrowing, sighing, bleeding, dying
Sealed in the stone-cold tomb

5.

Glorious now behold Him arise
King and God and sacrifice
Alleluia, Alleluia
Earth to the heavens replies

Jolly Old St. Nicholas

(1870s)

1.

Jolly old Saint Nicholas,
Lean your ear this way!
Don't you tell a single soul
What I'm going to say;
Christmas Eve is coming soon;
Now, you dear old man,
Whisper what you'll bring to me;
Tell me if you can.

2.

When the clock is striking twelve,
When I'm fast asleep,
Down the chimney broad and black,
With your pack you'll creep;
All the stockings you will find
Hanging in a row;
Mine will be the shortest one,
You'll be sure to know.

3.

Johnny wants a pair of skates;
Susy wants a dolly;
Nellie wants a story book;
She thinks dolls are folly;
As for me, my little brain
Isn't very bright;
Choose for me, old Santa Claus,
What you think is right.

Up on the Housetop

(1870s)

1.

Up on the housetop, reindeer pause
Out jumps good ol' Santa Claus
Down through the chimney with
    lots of toys
All for the little ones, Christmas joys
Ho, Ho, Ho! Who wouldn't go?
Ho, Ho, Ho! Who wouldn't go?
Up on the housetop, click, click, click
Down through the chimney with
    good Saint Nick

2.

First comes the stocking of little Nell
Oh, dear Santa, fill it well
Give her a dolly that laughs and cries
One that will open and shut her eyes

Ho, Ho, Ho! Who wouldn't go?
Ho, Ho, Ho! Who wouldn't go?
Up on the housetop, click, click, click
Down through the chimney with good
Saint Nick

3.

Next comes the stocking of little Will
Oh, just see what a glorious fill
Here is a hammer and lots of tacks
Also a ball and a whip that cracks
Ho, Ho, Ho! Who wouldn't go?
Ho, Ho, Ho! Who wouldn't go?
Up on the housetop, click, click, click
Down through the chimney with good
Saint Nick

A Visit from St. Nicholas

BY CLEMENT CLARKE MOORE

'Twas the night before Christmas, when all
    through the house
Not a creature was stirring, not even a mouse;
The stockings were hung by the chimney with care,
In hopes that ST. NICHOLAS soon would be there;
The children were nestled all snug in their beds,
While visions of sugarplums danced in their heads;
And mamma in her 'kerchief, and I in my cap,
Had just settled our brains for a long winter's nap,
When out on the lawn there arose such a clatter,
I sprang from the bed to see what was the matter.
Away to the window I flew like a flash,
Tore open the shutters and threw up the sash.
The moon on the breast of the new-fallen snow
Gave the lustre of midday to objects below,
When, what to my wondering eyes should appear,
But a miniature sleigh, and eight tiny reindeer,
With a little old driver, so lively and quick,
I knew in a moment it must be St. Nick.
More rapid than eagles his coursers they came,
And he whistled, and shouted, and called them by name;
"Now, Dasher! now, Dancer! now, Prancer and Vixen!
On, Comet! on, Cupid! on, Donder and Blitzen!
To the top of the porch! to the top of the wall!
Now dash away! dash away! dash away all!"
As dry leaves that before the wild hurricane fly,
When they meet with an obstacle, mount to the sky;

So up to the housetop the coursers they flew,
With the sleigh full of Toys, and St. Nicholas too.
And then, in a twinkling, I heard on the roof
The prancing and pawing of each little hoof.
As I drew in my head, and was turning around,
Down the chimney St. Nicholas came with a bound.
He was dressed all in fur, from his head to his foot,
And his clothes were all tarnished with ashes and soot;
A bundle of Toys he had flung on his back,
And he looked like a peddler just opening his pack.
His eyes—how they twinkled! his dimples how merry!
His cheeks were like roses, his nose like a cherry!
His droll little mouth was drawn up like a bow
And the beard of his chin was as white as the snow;
The stump of a pipe he held tight in his teeth,
And the smoke it encircled his head like a wreath;
He had a broad face and a little round belly,
That shook when he laughed, like a bowlful of jelly.

He was chubby and plump, a right jolly old elf,
And I laughed when I saw him, in spite of myself;
A wink of his eye and a twist of his head,
Soon gave me to know I had nothing to dread;
He spoke not a word, but went straight to his work,
And filled all the stockings; then turned with a jerk,
And laying his finger aside of his nose,
And giving a nod, up the chimney he rose;
He sprang to his sleigh, to his team gave a whistle,
And away they all flew like the down of a thistle,
But I heard him exclaim, ere he drove out of sight,
"Happy Christmas to all, and to all a good-night."

THE GIFT
OF THE MAGI

BY O. HENRY

One dollar and eighty-seven cents. That was all. And sixty cents of it was in pennies. Pennies saved one and two at a time by bull-dozing the grocer and the vegetable man and the butcher until one's cheeks burned with the silent imputation of parsimony that such close dealing implied. Three times Della counted it. One dollar and eighty- seven cents. And the next day would be Christmas.

There was clearly nothing to do but flop down on the shabby little couch and howl. So Della did it. Which instigates the moral reflection that life is made up of sobs, sniffles, and smiles, with sniffles predominating.

While the mistress of the home is gradually subsiding from the first stage to the second, take a look at the home. A furnished flat at $8 per week. It did not exactly beggar description, but it certainly had that word on the lookout for the mendicancy squad.

In the vestibule below was a letter-box into which no letter would go, and an electric button from which no mortal finger could coax a ring. Also appertaining thereunto was a card bearing the name "Mr. James Dillingham Young."

The "Dillingham" had been flung to the breeze during a former period of prosperity when its possessor was being paid $30 per week. Now, when the income was shrunk to $20, though, they were thinking seriously of contracting to a modest and unassuming D. But whenever Mr. James Dillingham Young came home and reached his flat above he was called "Jim" and greatly hugged by Mrs. James Dillingham Young, already introduced to you as Della. Which is all very good.

Della finished her cry and attended to her cheeks with the powder rag. She stood by the window and looked out dully at a gray cat walking a gray fence in a gray backyard. Tomorrow would be Christmas Day, and she had only $1.87 with which to buy Jim a present. She had been saving every penny she could for months, with this result. Twenty dollars a week doesn't go far. Expenses had been greater than she had calculated. They always are. Only $1.87 to buy a present for Jim. Her Jim. Many a happy hour she had spent planning for something nice for him. Something fine and rare and sterling—something just a little bit near to being worthy of the honor of being owned by Jim.

There was a pier glass between the windows of the room. Perhaps you have seen a pier glass in an $8 flat. A very thin and very agile person may, by observing his reflection in a rapid sequence of longitudinal strips, obtain a fairly accurate conception of his looks. Della, being slender, had mastered the art.

Suddenly she whirled from the window and stood before the glass. Her eyes were shining brilliantly, but her face had lost its color within twenty seconds. Rapidly she pulled down her hair and let it fall to its full length.

Now, there were two possessions of the James Dillingham Youngs in which they both took a mighty pride. One was Jim's gold watch that had been his father's and his grandfather's. The other was Della's hair. Had the queen of Sheba lived in the flat across the airshaft, Della would have let her hair hang out the window some day to dry just to depreciate Her Majesty's jewels and gifts. Had King Solomon been the janitor, with all his treasures piled up in the basement, Jim would have pulled out his watch every time he passed, just to see him pluck at his beard from envy.

So now Della's beautiful hair fell about her rippling and shining like a cascade of brown waters. It reached below her knee and made itself almost a garment for her. And then she did it up again nervously and quickly. Once she faltered for a minute and stood still while a tear or two splashed on the worn red carpet.

On went her old brown jacket; on went her old brown hat. With a whirl of skirts and with the brilliant sparkle still in her eyes, she fluttered out the door and down the stairs to the street.

Where she stopped the sign read: "Mme. Sofronie. Hair Goods of All Kinds." One flight up Della ran, and collected herself, panting. Madame, large, too white, chilly, hardly looked the "Sofronie."

"Will you buy my hair?" asked Della.

"I buy hair," said Madame. "Take yer hat off and let's have a sight at the looks of it."

Down rippled the brown cascade.

"Twenty dollars," said Madame, lifting the mass with a practised hand.

"Give it to me quick," said Della.

Oh, and the next two hours tripped by on rosy wings. Forget the hashed metaphor. She was ransacking the stores for Jim's present.

She found it at last. It surely had been made for Jim and no one else. There was no other like it in any of the stores, and she had turned all of them inside out. It was a platinum fob chain simple and chaste in design, properly proclaiming its value by substance alone and not by meretricious ornamentation—as all good things should do. It was even worthy of The Watch. As soon as she saw it she knew that it must be Jim's. It was like him. Quietness and value—the description applied to both. Twenty-one dollars they took from her for it, and she hurried home with the 87 cents. With that chain on his watch Jim might be properly anxious about the time in any company. Grand as the watch was, he sometimes looked at it on the sly on account of the old leather strap that he used in place of a chain.

When Della reached home her intoxication gave way a little to prudence and reason. She got out her curling irons and lighted the gas and went to work repairing the ravages made by generosity added to love. Which is always a tremendous task, dear friends—a mammoth task.

Within forty minutes her head was covered with tiny, close-lying curls that made her look wonderfully like a truant schoolboy. She looked at her reflection in the mirror long, carefully, and critically.

"If Jim doesn't kill me," she said to herself, "before he takes a second look at me, he'll say I look like a Coney Island chorus girl. But what could I do—oh! what could I do with a dollar and eighty- seven cents?"

At 7 o'clock the coffee was made and the frying-pan was on the back of the stove hot and ready to cook the chops.

Jim was never late. Della doubled the fob chain in her hand and sat on the corner of the table near the door that he always entered. Then she heard his step on the stair away down on the first flight, and she turned white for just a moment. She had a habit of saying little silent prayers about the simplest everyday things, and now she whispered: "Please God, make him think I am still pretty."

The door opened and Jim stepped in and closed it. He looked thin and very serious. Poor fellow, he was only twenty-two—and to be burdened with a family! He needed a new overcoat and he was without gloves.

Jim stopped inside the door, as immovable as a setter at the scent of quail. His eyes were fixed upon Della, and there was an expression in them that she could not read, and it terrified her. It was not anger, nor surprise, nor disapproval, nor horror, nor any of the sentiments that she had been prepared for. He simply stared at her fixedly with that peculiar expression on his face.

Della wriggled off the table and went for him.

"Jim, darling," she cried, "don't look at me that way. I had my hair cut off and sold because I couldn't have lived through Christmas without giving you a present. It'll grow out again—you won't mind, will you? I just had to do it. My hair grows awfully fast. Say 'Merry Christmas!' Jim, and let's be happy. You don't know what a nice—what a beautiful, nice gift I've got for you."

"You've cut off your hair?" asked Jim, laboriously, as if he had not arrived at that patent fact yet even after the hardest mental labor.

"Cut it off and sold it," said Della. "Don't you like me just as well, anyhow? I'm me without my hair, ain't I?"

Jim looked about the room curiously.

"You say your hair is gone?" he said, with an air almost of idiocy.

"You needn't look for it," said Della. "It's sold, I tell you—sold and gone, too. It's Christmas Eve, boy. Be good to me, for it went for you. Maybe the hairs of my head were numbered," she went on with sudden serious sweetness, "but nobody could ever count my love for you. Shall I put the chops on, Jim?"

Out of his trance Jim seemed quickly to wake. He enfolded his Della. For ten seconds let us regard with discreet scrutiny some inconsequential object in the other direction. Eight dollars a week or a million a year—what is the difference? A mathematician or a wit would give you the wrong answer. The magi brought valuable gifts, but that was not

among them. This dark assertion will be illuminated later on.

Jim drew a package from his overcoat pocket and threw it upon the table.

"Don't make any mistake, Dell," he said, "about me. I don't think there's anything in the way of a haircut or a shave or a shampoo that could make me like my girl any less. But if you'll unwrap that package you may see why you had me going a while at first."

White fingers and nimble tore at the string and paper. And then an ecstatic scream of joy; and then, alas! a quick feminine change to hysterical tears and wails, necessitating the immediate employment of all the comforting powers of the lord of the flat.

For there lay The Combs—the set of combs, side and back, that Della had worshipped long in a Broadway window. Beautiful combs, pure tortoise shell, with jewelled rims—just the shade to wear in the beautiful vanished hair. They were expensive combs, she knew, and her heart had simply craved and yearned over them without the least hope of possession. And now, they were hers, but the tresses that should have adorned the coveted adornments were gone.

But she hugged them to her bosom, and at length she was able to look up with dim eyes and a smile and say: "My hair grows so fast, Jim!"

And then Della leaped up like a little singed cat and cried, "Oh, oh!"

Jim had not yet seen his beautiful present. She held it out to him eagerly upon her open palm. The dull precious metal seemed to flash with a reflection of her bright and ardent spirit.

"Isn't it a dandy, Jim? I hunted all over town to find it. You'll have to look at the time a hundred times a day now. Give me your watch. I want to see how it looks on it."

Instead of obeying, Jim tumbled down on the couch and put his hands under the back of his head and smiled.

"Dell," said he, "let's put our Christmas presents away and keep 'em a while. They're too nice to use just at present. I sold the watch to get the money to buy your combs. And now suppose you put the chops on."

The magi, as you know, were wise men —wonderfully wise men—who brought gifts to the Babe in the manger. They invented the art of giving Christmas presents. Being wise, their gifts were no doubt wise ones, possibly bearing the privilege of exchange in case of duplication. And here I have lamely related to you the uneventful chronicle of two foolish children in a flat who most unwisely sacrificed for each other the greatest treasures of their house. But in a last word to the wise of these days let it be said that of all who give gifts these two were the wisest. Of all who give and receive gifts, such as they are wisest. Everywhere they are wisest. They are the magi.

PINE WREATH

Every family has its own holiday traditions. For some, Christmas truly arrives only when the tree ornaments are first unpacked. Others could not imagine an Easter without mixing dyes and making decorated eggs. And everyone knows the joy of receiving a valentine from someone special. We can channel our creative urges to re-create familiar images from our childhood or to build new visions of important traditions.

Nothing evokes the warm feelings of Christmas quite so effectively as a traditional evergreen wreath with its broad red ribbon. Depending on your preferences, you can construct this wreath with natural or artificial greenery. To build a quick evergreen base, wind a garland of fir or spruce around a wire wreath form, securing it periodically with wire. Flatten a spot on the greens, and wire a small, square piece of foam onto the base. You can disguise the foam by gluing sheet moss over it. Using about four yards (3.5 m) of velvet ribbon, tie a bow and pick it into the foam. Then pick four natural mahogany pods and approximately two feet (61 cm) of silk grape-leaf ivy into the foam. To add color and texture, wind a few red berry tips onto the ends of the silk ivy, and attach pine cone rosettes in a few locations around the wreath. For a whimsical touch, glue or wire a red-feathered bird onto one of the branches.

TRADITIONAL BERRY WREATH

Traditional Christmas colors highlight this small, easy-to-make wreath that could be used as a wall or door decoration or set around a candle as a table centerpiece. Start with a purchased base of artificial greenery and hot-glue first a layer of German statice, then a circle of pepperberries around the surface.

SANTA WREATH

Some wreaths start with an attractive base. Others begin with an idea. This one was inspired by a rosy-cheeked, ceramic Santa Claus face that seems perfectly framed in its halo of ribbon and greenery. Look over your own collection of Christmas treasures—it might inspire a new life for an old decoration. This wreath was made by first attaching a 2 ¹/4" by 4" (5.7 by 10 cm) block of styrofoam to an 18" (45 cm) vine base with hot glue and wire. Stems of vinyl spruce branches were stuck into the foam with the greenery spread out across the upper right half of the base. The Santa face was wired to the base. Then a bow of red plaid ribbon was secured above his head with streamers weaved through the spruce and hot-glued to the base. Artificial berries and apples were hot-glued randomly through the greens along with dried globe amaranth, small dried mushrooms, and twigs.

EVERGREEN SWAG

This handsome door swag is too heavy to rely on foam alone for support. The designer hot-glued a long rectangle of two-inch-thick green Styrofoam (5 cm) to a sturdy board; the foam provided a means of anchoring the greenery, and the board supplied the necessary backing.

After he built the support, the designer secured a brass trumpet to the foam with an electrical conduit clamp. Branches of Fraser fir, picked into the foam, established the general shape. Then he filled in the center with short pieces of fir, eucalyptus, and boxwood. Dried pomegranates, cones, celosia, and wheat, picked in bunches, add interesting detail, along with a bow and streamers of Hunter green grosgrain ribbon.

TOLE PAINTED NATIVITY

Paint Palette:

Delta:

Black
Black Green
Blue Spruce
Burnt Sienna
Burnt Umber
Chamomile
Charcoal
Dark Brown
Dark Burnt Umber
Drizzle Grey
Flesh: Dark, Medium
Flesh Tan
Ivory
Leprechaun
Light Ivory
Maple Sugar
Mudstone
Palomino
Pine Green
Quaker Grey
Rain Grey
Raw Sienna
Rouge
Sandstone
Spice Brown
Spice Tan
Storm Grey
Terra Cotta
Territorial Beige
Trail

Victorian Teal:

Dark, Light, Medium
Wedgewood Green
White

Supplies:

Wooden Nativity with Manger

All Faces and Hands:

1. Base faces, necks, hands, and wrists with Medium Flesh. Shade with Dark Flesh.

2. Blush cheeks and noses with Rouge.

3. Line eyes with Black and mouths with Dark Flesh + Rouge. Line eyebrows with Burnt Umber.

4. Line some hair across foreheads (except on Baby Jesus) with shades of Dark Brown, Burnt Umber, and Dark Burnt Umber.

Shepherd:

Note: Using a chalk pencil, draw robes and drapes on figures. After basing, add folds and wrinkles on appropriate articles of clothing.

1. Base gown with Trail. Shade with Territorial Beige, then again with Dark Brown. Highlight neckline with Trail + Light Ivory.

2. Base one small and one large stripe around bottom of gown with Burnt Sienna. Dry-brush through center of large stripe with Terra Cotta. Base stripes on sleeves and neck with Burnt Sienna.

3. Base belt with Dark Brown.

4. Base drape with Flesh Tan. Shade with Palomino. Highlight with Ivory.

5. Base headdress with Spice Brown.

6. Base stripes on headdress with Burnt Umber + Glazing Medium. Dry-brush highlight between stripes with Territorial Beige.

7. Base headband with Burnt Sienna. Dry-brush lines with Terra Cotta. Shade next to head-band with Dark Burnt Umber.

Mary:

1. Base gown with Sandstone. Stipple with Sandstone + Light Ivory, then again with Light Ivory. Shade with Mudstone, then again with Mudstone a small amount of Dark Burnt Umber.

2. Base robe and headdress with Dark Victorian Teal. Highlight robe with Medium Victorian Teal, then again with Light Victorian Teal. Shade with Blue Spruce, then again with Blue Spruce + Black Green.

3. Base both stripes along bottoms of head-dress and headband with Chamomile. Shade with Spice Tan. Highlight with Light Ivory.

4. Base belt and trim along edge of robe with Blue Spruce. Shade with Blue Spruce + Black Green. Highlight with Medium Victorian Teal.

Joseph:

1. Base gown with Quaker Grey. Stipple with Quaker Grey + White. Shade with Rain Grey, then again with Storm Grey.

2. Base robe with Pine Green. Highlight with Leprechaun, then again with Wedgewood Green. Shade with Black Green.

3. Base stripe near bottom of robe with Spice Tan. Shade with Raw Sienna. Highlight with Maple Sugar.

4. Base belt with Spice Tan. Add tiny "S" strokes with Burnt Sienna. Highlight between strokes with Maple Sugar.

5. Base headdress with Rain Grey. Highlight with Quaker Grey, then again with Drizzle Grey.

6. Base stripes on headdress with Rain Grey + Storm Grey + Glazing Medium 2:1:1. Shade with Charcoal. Stipple one stripe on headdress with Pine Green.

7. Base headband with Charcoal. Add "S" strokes with Drizzle Grey + Pine Green. Highlight with Drizzle Grey + Pine Green + White.

Baby Jesus:

1. Wash over hair area with a Dark Brown wash. Line some curls on hair with Dark Brown + Burnt Umber. Darken with Dark Burnt Umber.

2. Base body with Light Ivory. Shade with Mudstone. Highlight with White.

Note: If desired, Baby Jesus can be wrapped in a small piece of fabric or felt.

Manger:

1. Lightly wash manger with Spice Brown so wood grain shows through. Shade with Burnt Umber.

2. To create three wood planks on sides of manger, shade with Dark Burnt Umber. Dry-brush through centers with Raw Sienna.

3. To create nails, apply dots on corner supports with Burnt Umber.

CHRISTMAS TREE SANTA

Dana Irwin based this figure on an antique ornament that has been in her family for generations. Using a ribbon sash around his waist, the Santa is tied into the Christmas tree and nestled among the branches.

Materials & Tools

- small-gauge chicken wire
- needle-nose pliers
- wire cutter
- small piece quilted fabric
- needle and thread
- instant papier-mâché
- plastic wrap
- rolling pin
- modeling tool
- ⅓ yd. (30.5 cm) red felt
- polyester beard material, fur, or lamb's wool
- acrylic paints
- artist's brush
- herb sprig
- 1 ⅔ yds. (1.5 m) narrow fabric ribbon
- clear glitter
- glue gun

Instructions

1. Crush the chicken wire into the rough shape of a head, body, and arms (fig. 1). Use the wire cutter as needed to separate portions of the wire to form the arms and turn one arm upward with the pliers.

2. To give Santa a rounded figure, wrap a piece of quilted fabric around the body por-

tion of the armature and tack it in place with needle and thread.

3. Prepare the instant papier-mâché according to the package instructions. Place a ball of pulp between two pieces of plastic wrap and flatten it into a sheet about ¼" (6 mm) thick using the rolling pin. Wrap portions of the sheet over the head and hands, smoothing them with dampened fingers. Allow this layer to dry overnight.

4. Using small dabs of papier-mâché, form the facial features and shape the hands. Dampen your fingers or modeling tool before using it to prevent the pulp from sticking. Don't worry if the face and hands aren't perfectly smooth; the rough texture adds to the aged appearance.

5. While the papier-mâché is drying, cut the pattern pieces for the hooded robe, as indicated in figure 2. Be sure to add seam allowances and hems where necessary. Sew the side and shoulder seams of the robe and the front and back seams of the hood, leaving the bottom front open. Then sew the hood to the neck, easing any fullness at the neck.

6. When the papier-mâché is completely dry, paint the face and hands with acrylic paints. The eyes are the most distinct feature and most important. Figure 3 shows one method for painting the eyes.

7. In the original antique version, Santa's beard is made of fur, and the Santa pictured here has a beard made of polyester fibers. Using either of these or lamb's wool, hot-glue a beard to Santa's face.

8. Glue an herb sprig in one hand and attach a ribbon around Santa's waist, leaving the long ends free to tie around the Christmas tree. Then give him a sprinkling of snow on the shoulders and head by gluing clear glitter to his robe.

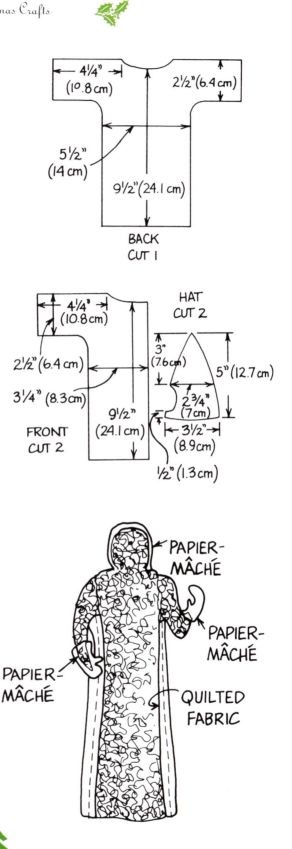

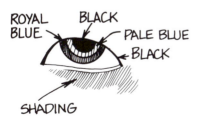

PAINTED EGG ORNAMENTS

Pat Scheible creates family heirlooms from all types of eggs—chicken, cockatoo, goose, or quail. The outside surfaces are hand painted, and the insides contain tiny dioramas with festive themes.

Materials & Tools

- *infertile egg of your choice*
- *needle*
- *fine manicure scissors or motorized "mini-tool"*
- *lighted magnifying glass*
- *acrylic paints*
- *artist's brushes*
- *onion skins, white and purple*
- *stylus with sharp point*
- *spray matte acrylic sealer*
- *German N-gauge model railroad figurines*
- *white glue*
- *decorative ribbon trim*
- *pendant finding*

Instructions

Pierce the ends of the egg with a needle and blow out the contents.

If you want to make a diorama, you must soften the shell before cutting it. Soak the shell in water overnight; then cut an oval hole in one side with the manicure scissors or "mini-tool."

Begin your diorama by painting the background image. The area is small and fragile,

so you won't be able to make a sketch. Using a lighted magnifying glass to help you see, paint the area with a fine artist's brush and acrylic paints.

Paint the miniature figurines with the colors of your choice. Then set these aside until you finish with the outside of the shell.

Transfer one of the designs in figure 1 or create a new image by sketching very lightly on the shell with a soft pencil. Add paint in blocks of color, starting with the main figure and finishing with smaller details.

If you want to make a reverse image like that on the brown egg, first boil the egg with a generous quantity of onion skins for about

two hours. A light chalk outline of your figure may be useful, but it's likely to smudge as you work. Using a sharp stylus, gently scratch the image in a series of small strokes. The closer you place your scratches, the lighter the area will become. This is the opposite effect of normal drawing, so you may want to try it on a few practice eggs first.

Once your scratched image is complete, spray the entire outside surface of the egg with two or three coats of clear matte sealer.

Now complete your diorama by installing the figurines and other items, such as trees made from stems of herbs, paper buildings, or cotton snow. Tiny dabs of white glue are sufficient to hold them in place.

Hide the cut edge by gluing a piece of ribbon trim around the opening.

Finish your ornament by gluing a pendant finding onto the top of the egg.

FIGURE 1

CLASSIC GINGERBREAD HOUSE

If you're a traditionalist, it's hard to beat a design like this one—dripping with sugar and icing and candy décor. The delight is in the details, plus the polished finishing touches, from stenciled designs iced onto windows and the mosaic-like front path of candy fruits to the twinkling gumdrops on the ridges of the roofs.

The snowman in the yard sparkles when the light hits him, as if his body is made of real packed snow. The process for making one is simple, and the result is a sturdy decoration. Pack granulated sugar and a few drops of water into tablespoon-size measuring spoons. Let these half balls dry (and harden) into shape, then ice them together for perfectly formed snowballs. Create as many as you need—and build away.

Create a neat little picket fence using a technique similar to the one described above for the snowman. Fence molds are available at shops that carry cake decorating supplies. Pack them with the same sugar-and-water-drop mixture, then immediately dump the molded sugar onto a flat surface covered with wax paper. Your fence pieces should be dry in a couple of hours.

Red licorice pieces mortared into place

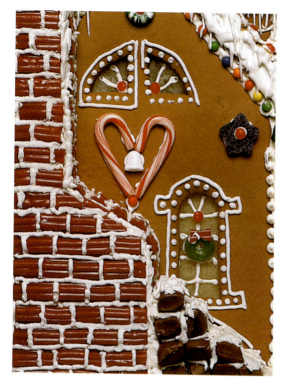

make a perfectly uniform brick chimney. Tootsie Rolls covered with royal icing snow form an ideal log pile to lean up against it.

A shingling style like this, using layered wafer cookies and accents of Red Hots, takes a little time and a careful eye, but the attention to detail adds loads of charm.

Don't forgo the research process (that is, strolling the aisles of candy stores) advises Sally Fredrickson and many other gingerbread house builders. It's the only way to spot licorice dogs, little candy boots, bells, lanterns, and other accents you need to make your gingerbread house a home.

EGGNOG

This is the traditional, simple eggnog recipe.

1 free-range egg
1 oz / 3 cL brandy
1 oz / 3 cL dark rum
3 oz / 9 cL milk
1 tbsp gomme syrup

Pour all ingredients, except milk, into a shaker. Shake. Strain into a goblet. Stir in the milk. Grate fresh nutmeg on top.

HOT BUTTERED RUM

A classic with a spicy finish, this is a little fattening for those on a diet, but worth every mouthful.

1 $2/3$ oz / 5 cL dark rum
1 slice soft butter
1 teaspoon brown sugar
1 small cinnamon stick
1 pinch grated nutmeg
4 drops vanilla extract
2 oz / 6 cL boiling water

Mix the butter, brown sugar, cinnamon, nutmeg, and vanilla extract in a heatproof wine glass until creamed. Add the rum and the boiling water. Stir. Serve hot.

Chapter Two

VICTORIAN CHRISTMAS

• • • • • • • • • • • • •

Perhaps the most influential historical period on Christmas culture and customs, the Victorian Era and its deep British roots continue to inspire Christmas celebrations. A Victorian Christmas is often associated with carolers dressed in long overcoats and shiny top hats, romantic bows, golden cherubs, and the glow of candles. Recreate your own Victorian Christmas with a selection of favorite carols, many of which were English from long before Queen Victoria. Wrap your presents, decorate your home, and trim your tree with Victorian-inspired materials, colors, and fabrics. Extend the Victorian theme into the kitchen by creating scenes out of a Brontë or Dickens novel with the lovely gingerbread houses ranging from the Avonlea Inn— a beautiful Victorian house, to the romantic Candlelit Cottage to the quaint Coventry Alley. Let the romance and the charm of the Victorian Era inspire Christmas cheer and warm memories!

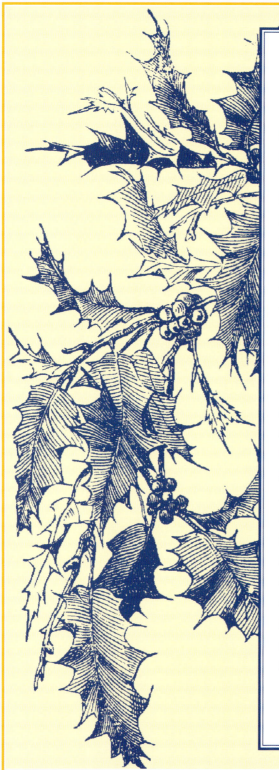

Deck the Halls

(M. ANCIENT WELSH, 1800S)

1.

Deck the halls with boughs of holly
Fa la la la la la la la la
'Tis the season to be jolly
Fa la la la la la la la la
Fill the mead cup, drain the barrel
Fa la la la la la la la la
Troll the ancient Yuletide carol
Fa la la la la la la la la

2.

See the flowing bowl before us
Fa la la la la la la la la
Strike the harp and join the chorus
Fa la la la la la la la la
Follow me in merry measure
Fa la la la la la la la la
While I sing of beauty's treasure
Fa la la la la la la la la

3.

Fast away the old year passes
Fa la la la la la la la la
Hail the new ye lads and lasses
Fa la la la la la la la la
Laughing, quaffing, all altogether
Fa la la la la la la la la
Heedless of the wind and weather
Fa la la la la la la la la

O Come All Ye Faithful

(1751)

1.

O come all ye faithful
Joyful and triumphant
O come ye, O come ye to Bethlehem
Come and behold him
Born the King of Angels

Refrain:

O come, let us adore Him
O come, let us adore Him
O come, let us adore Him
Christ the Lord

2.

Sing choirs of Angels
Sing in exultation
Sing all ye citizens of heav'n above
Sing ye "All glory
to God in the highest"

3.

Yea, Lord we greet Thee
Born this happy morning
Jesus, to Thee be all glory given
Word of the Father
Now in flesh appearing

Hark, the Herald Angels Sing

(1855)

1.

Hark! The herald angels sing
Glory to the newborn King
Peace on earth and mercy mild
God and sinners reconciled
Joyful, all ye nations, rise
Join the triumph of the skies
With the angelic host proclaim
"Christ is born in Bethlehem"
Hark the herald angels sing
Glory to the newborn King

2.

Christ, by highest heaven adored
Christ the everlasting Lord
Late in time behold him come
Offspring of a Virgin's womb
Veiled in flesh the Godhead see!
Hail, the incarnate Deity!
Pleased as man with man to dwell
Jesus our Emmanuel
Hark the herald angels sing
Glory to the newborn King

3.

Hail, the heaven-born Prince of peace!
Hail, the Sun of righteousness!
Light and life to all He brings
Risen with healing in His wings
Mild He lays His glory by
Born that man no more may die
Born to raise the sons of earth
Born to give them second birth
Hark the herald angels sing
Glory to the newborn King

The Holly and the Ivy

(1700)

1.

The holly and the ivy
When they are both full grown
Of all the trees that are in the wood
The holly wears the crown

Refrain:

The rising of the sun
And the running of the deer
The playing of the merry organ
Sweet singing in the choir

2.

The holly bears a blossom
As white as lily flower
And Mary bore sweet Jesus Christ
To be our sweet Saviour

3.

The holly bears a berry
As red as any blood
And Mary bore sweet Jesus Christ
To do poor sinners good

4.

The holly bears a prickle
As sharp as any thorn
And Mary bore sweet Jesus Christ
On Christmas day in the morn

5.

The holly bears a bark
As bitter as any gall
And Mary bore sweet Jesus Christ
For to redeem us all

Come, O Come, Emmanuel

(1800)

1.

O come, O come, Emmanuel
And ransom captive Israel
That mourns in lonely exile here
Until the Son of God appear
Rejoice! Rejoice! Emmanuel
Shall come to thee, O Israel.

2.

O come, Thou Rod of Jesse, free
Thine own from Satan's tyranny
From depths of Hell Thy people save
And give them victory o'er the grave
Rejoice! Rejoice! Emmanuel
Shall come to thee, O Israel.

3.

O come, Thou Day-Spring, come and cheer
Our spirits by Thine advent here
Disperse the gloomy clouds of night
And death's dark shadows put to flight.
Rejoice! Rejoice! Emmanuel
Shall come to thee, O Israel.

4.

O come, Thou Key of David, come,
And open wide our heavenly home;
Make safe the way that leads on high,
And close the path to misery.
Rejoice! Rejoice! Emmanuel
Shall come to thee, O Israel.

5.

O come, O come, Thou Lord of might,
Who to Thy tribes, on Sinai's height,
In ancient times did'st give the Law,
In cloud, and majesty and awe.
Rejoice! Rejoice! Emmanuel
Shall come to thee, O Israel.

We Wish You a Merry Christmas

(AT LEAST 1500s)

We wish you a Merry Christmas;
We wish you a Merry Christmas;
We wish you a Merry Christmas
    and a Happy New Year.
Good tidings we bring to you
    and your kin;
Good tidings for Christmas
    and a Happy New Year.

Oh, bring us a figgy pudding;
Oh, bring us a figgy pudding;

Oh, bring us a figgy pudding and a
    cup of good cheer
We won't go until we get some;
We won't go until we get some;
We won't go until we get some,
    so bring some out here

We wish you a Merry Christmas;
We wish you a Merry Christmas;
We wish you a Merry Christmas
    and a Happy New Year.

VICTORIAN WRAPS

One of the best trends in gift wrapping is the appearance of festive tote bags. They range in size from substantial to minuscule, ready to hold a VCR or a single truffle. This one is even more attractive than most. A corsage made of dried roses, pink-dyed peppergrass, sprays of pepperberries, and sprigs of boxwood is hot-glued to the bag.

Wrapped in pink moiré paper, this elegant package will shine under the tree. A silver bow forms the center of the decoration, with materials hot-glued on each side: artemisia, dusty miller, celosia, dyed German statice, dyed peppergrass, and bunches of della robia grapes.

This pink metallic bow is wired and ready to turn a mundane package into an occasion. The bow requires four feet (1.2 m) of 1 1/2" wide (3.75 cm) ribbon. Leaving one tail 11 inches (27.5 cm) long and the other 19 inches (47.5 cm) long, form a bow with six loops (three on each side) and wire it in the center, after pulling the tails into place. Leave enough wire to attach to a package's ribbon. Cut a disc of clear, lightweight plastic (check the kitchen) and glue it to the front of the bow, to serve as a base for the naturals. Working from the outside to the center, hot-glue the herbs and flowers onto the plastic disc: bay leaves, caspia, yarrow, lavender, statice, celosia, thistle, globe amaranth, and strawflowers.

The elongated blooms of rattail celosia are the attention-getters on this small package. Also hot-glued to the pink moiré paper are boxwood, dyed peppergrass, and della robia fruit.

The square red package is decorated with pine cones, cinnamon sticks, star anise, and boxwood, hot-glued to the paper.

VICTORIAN FATHER CHRISTMAS

Our Victorian Era forebears had a tendency to take their holidays with a greater degree of seriousness than we do today. Mary Beth Ruby reflects this perspective in a rather dour Santa who's seen perhaps one too many empty stockings awaiting him.

Materials & Tools

instant papier-mâché
plastic wrap
rolling pin
12" (30.5 cm) polystyrene cone
craft knife
modeling tools
acrylic paints
artist's brushes
acrylic matte varnish
self-stick felt

Instructions

1. Mix the instant papier-mâché according to the manufacturer's instructions. Place a ball of the pulp between two sheets of plastic wrap and flatten it into a sheet about ⅛" (3 mm) thick with the rolling pin.

2. After first dampening your fingers, smooth the sheet onto the cone. Then allow it to dry for a day or two.

3. Flatten additional sheets of papier-mâché and cut them into pieces for the arms, beard, fur trim, and hat. For the facial features and teddy bear, apply small bits of pulp

with your damp fingers. Then smooth and refine them with the modeling tool. Using the same tool, make long vertical grooves in the beard and hair. Don't worry about any small cracks and bumps; these will help make your figure look more like an antique.

4. After the papier-mâché has dried completely, paint your Santa with acrylic paints. To dull the bright acrylic colors and give your figure an antique appearance, apply a thin coating of well-diluted burnt umber acrylic paint. Before it dries, wipe off the excess paint with a rag or paper towel. Seal the painted surface with a coat of acrylic varnish.

5. Cover the bottom of the cone with a circle of self-stick felt.

PINE, FRUIT AND GOLD WREATH

Gold ranks right behind red and green in the triumvirate of traditional Christmas colors. But it is also a favorite autumn tone, making this wreath an appropriate decoration throughout the Thanksgiving/harvest season as well. It was made by first weaving and twisting olive and gold velvet ribbons through the branches of a silk Canadian pine wreath. Next a green bow was hot-glued on at the bottom. Finally, holiday picks tipped with cones, gold berries, bronze fruit, gold leaves, and ornaments were hot-glued into place.

VIOLIN AND CHERUB WREATH

Here's an attractive wreath that is sure to attract roving Christmas carolers to your door. The designer used a gilded violin, singing cherubs, and stave-printed ribbon to weave a musical theme through this colorful composition of natural and artificial flora. She first wrapped a wire form with green garland and wired the violin into place. Cloth ribbon was laid over crepe paper, tied into a bow and wired to the base. A magnolia blossom, gold-painted leaves, yarrow, sumac flowers, and baby's breath (also sprayed gold) were attached with hot glue, as were the golden angels.

48

COPPER RIBBON WREATH

Glittering copper ribbon and matte green leaves—contrasting colors and surfaces make this table wreath an intriguing centerpiece. The designer covered the straw base with protea leaves, picking them at an angle so that they overlap well. She then taped plastic candleholders onto the base. Next came wispy plumosa fern, hot-glued between the leaves. She gave the wreath two bows: first a large one of copper-foil ribbon, then a smaller one on top. Finally, she hot-glued white parchment flowers around the bow and inserted the candles.

DECORATE YOUR HOME FOR A VICTORIAN CHRISTMAS

❧ Adorn a serving tray with Victorian-inspired objects such as a porcelain cherub or a pretty book. And for a unique twist, use a glass goblet as a candlestick.

❧ Decorate throw pillows with festive gold and cream ribbons and bows. Add a touch of elegance with Christmas angels and antique linens.

❧ Dress up a Christmas tree using hand-made harlequin ornaments with gold tassels, white bows, and gold wire ribbon. Subtly continue the theme by using the same ribbon on the tree and the presents.

❧ Fill a glass bowl halfway with marbles and add a large gold candle to create a merry, eye-pleasing decoration. Surround the candle with beloved objects for a lovely effect.

ROLLED BEESWAX CANDLES

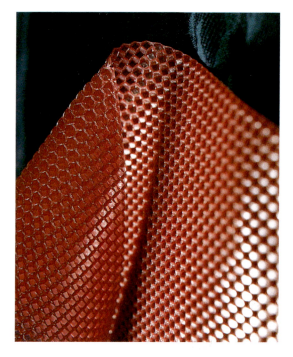

Candlesticks are nothing without candles, and these classy tapers are five-minute projects. Sheets of beeswax in various colors and spools of wicking are available at well-stocked craft stores. Store the candles at room temperature out of direct sunlight.

Materials

Sheet of beeswax
Wick

Tools

Sharp craft knife
Metal ruler (optional)

1. Bring the wax sheets to warm room temperature: 75° to 80° F (23° to 26° C). If they're too cool, the sheets will be brittle and hard to roll.

2. Cut a wick 1 inch (2.5 cm) longer than the candle will be tall. Lay it along one edge of the wax sheet, with the extra length at the top. See figure 1.

3. Carefully fold about ¼ inch (6 mm) of wax over the wick and gently mash it down.

4. Roll up the candle, keeping it as tightly rolled as possible without mashing the honeycomb pattern. If you need more than one sheet, butt the second up against the first, or overlap them and press them together into the thickness of a single sheet.

5. When the candle is as thick as you want, cut off the remaining beeswax sheet, using the ruler as a straightedge if desired. Gently press the cut edge into the body of the candle.

FIGURE 1

VICTORIAN ORNAMENTS

Paint Palettes:

Delta:

Apple Green
Black Cherry
Black Green
Chocolate Cherry
Forest Green
Raspberry
Seminole
White

Gleams:

Pearl Finish

Supplies:

Wooden Ornaments (4)
Circle Template

Note: Ornaments must be glued together prior to painting.

Dividing an Ornament into Sections:

Turn the ornament so you are looking directly down on the top. Using a chalk pencil, evenly divide the top into fourths. You can then further divide it into eighths or twelfths. Use these marks as reference points to create the designs.

Ornament #1:

1. Base-coat ornament with White, then again with two or three coats of Pearl Finish. Divide into eighths.

2. Base-coat cap with Black Cherry. Base stripe around center of cap with Raspberry.

3. Add one-strokes around top and bottom with Forest Green. Highlight "tips" with Apple Green. Dry-brush "tails" with Forest Green + Black Green.

4. Base-coat a broken stripe around center with Forest Green. Shade with Forest Green + Black Green. Reverse-float highlight with Apple Green.

5. Add descending dots between each stroke at top and bottom with Black Cherry. Highlight dots at top with a small amount of Raspberry.

10. For design connecting lower one-strokes, add a large dot above and between tops of one-strokes with Black Cherry. Highlight with a small amount of Raspberry. Add descending dots to encompass large dots with Raspberry. Add an "S" stroke on sides of each large dot with Black Cherry.

11. Add double-loaded reverse teardrops on sides of each large dot loaded with Apple Green and tipped with Forest Green. Add double-loaded reverse teardrops below each large dot loaded with Raspberry and tipped with Black Cherry.

Ornament #2:

1. Base-coat ornament with White, then again with two or three coats of Pearl Finish. Divide into twelfths.

2. Base-coat cap with Black Cherry.

3. Add elongated strokes around top with Forest Green. Dry-brush with Apple Green.

4. Add one-strokes in between elongated strokes with Black Cherry.

5. Add a large dot next to bottoms of elongated strokes with Forest Green. Add double-loaded reverse teardrops loaded with Raspberry and tipped with Black Cherry.

6. Base-coat stripe around center with Black Cherry.

7. Add descending dots on stripe with Pearl Finish.

6. Transfer Holly Pattern from below around ornament.

7. Base-coat holly leaves with Forest Green. Shade leaves and veins with Forest Green + Black Green. Highlight with Apple Green. Dot berries with Black Cherry. Highlight with Raspberry.

8. Add scrolls with Forest Green. Highlight with Apple Green.

9. Add double-loaded reverse teardrops above and below scrolls loaded with Apple Green and tipped with Forest Green. Add descending dots above and below scrolls with Raspberry.

8. Line "C" strokes below stripe with Forest Green. Add a large dot where each "C" connects with Raspberry.

9. Add double-loaded reverse teardrops below each large dot loaded with Raspberry and tipped with Black Cherry.

10. Add one-strokes around bottom with Black Cherry.

Ornament #3:

1. Base-coat ornament and cap with Forest Green. Divide into eighths.

2. Draw a ring around top approximately 5/8" down so all strokes end up the same length.

Note: This can be easily done by placing a circle template over ornament and drawing a circle with a chalk pencil.

3. Add spiraled strokes around top with Seminole. Shade behind right side of each stroke with Forest Green + Black Green. Dry-brush center of each stroke with Apple Green. Line top of each stroke with Forest Green + Black Green.

4. For design connecting upper spiraled strokes, add a large dot at bottom of each spiraled stroke with Black Cherry. Highlight with a small amount of Raspberry.

5. Add one-strokes with Pearl Finish.

6. Transfer Holly Pattern from below around ornament.

7. Base-coat holly leaves with Forest Green. Shade behind tops of leaves with Forest Green + Black Green. Highlight bottom edges of leaves with Apple Green. Dot berries with Black Cherry. Highlight with Raspberry.

8. Add scrolls and veins with Apple Green.

9. Add one-strokes below scrolls with Pearl Finish.

10. Add descending dots around ornament with Black Cherry. Add lines with Seminole. Highlight centers with Apple Green.

11. Add one-strokes around bottom with Pearl Finish.

Ornament #4:

1. Base ornament and cap with Black Cherry. Divide into eighths.

2. Add double-loaded one-strokes around top loaded with Raspberry and tipped with Pearl Finish.

3. Transfer Holly Pattern from below around ornament.

4. Base holly leaves with Forest Green. Shade behind tops of leaves with Chocolate Cherry. Line upper edges of leaves with Pearl Finish. Highlight bottom edges of leaves with Apple Green.

5. Add scrolls and veins with Apple Green.

6. Add dots with Raspberry. Add one-strokes above and below scrolls with Pearl Finish.

7. Add lines around center with Raspberry. Add descending dots at tops of lines with Pearl Finish.

8. Add scrolls with Forest Green. Dry-brush centers of scrolls with Apple Green. Add a dot at end of each scroll with

Seminole. Highlight with a small amount of Apple Green. Add double-loaded one-strokes below scrolls loaded with Raspberry and tipped with Pearl Finish.

9. Add one-strokes around bottom with Pearl Finish.

PRISM ORNAMENTS

Christmas tree ornaments are ever-popular Christmas gifts. These are based on prisms for chandeliers (available at lighting and home improvement stores). After the tree is gone, they can hang in a sunny window, casting rainbows around the room.

63

Materials

Monofilament (fishing line)
Prism
10-inch (25 cm) length of chiffon-type ribbon
Strands of wispy fern
Dried flowers

Tools

Scissors
Glue gun

1. Cut a piece of monofilament 12 inches (30 cm) long. Thread it through the metal ring on top of the prism and tie the line in a double knot right against the ring, leaving two long ends.

2. Make a bow with the ribbon and tie it onto the prism with the long pieces of monofilament. Tie the ends of the monofilament together, to make a loop for hanging.

3. Hot-glue the fern and flowers to the center of the bow.

GLASS BALL ORNAMENTS

Ordinary glass Christmas balls can become distinctive ornaments with natural materials hot-glued to the outside and a bright bow tied to the hanger.

The red and white bouquet at left consists of German statice, globe amaranth, and celosia.

On the ornaments below, dusty miller leaves support dainty peppergrass, topped with pepperberries and strawflowers. The materials also include dusty miller, peppergrass, and strawflowers, but add celosia and a pink rose on top.

A leaf of dusty miller adorns the silver ball, topped with a sprig of blue salvia and a delphinium bloom. Silver ribbon ties it together. The blown glass ornament also holds dusty miller, topped with artemisia and delphinium. The wired blue ribbon makes an effective bow.

Glass balls filled with potpourri add scent Remove the metal hook and wire from the top of the ornament, fill the ball about a third full of potpourri, and reattach hook to top, using a drop of quick glue. Run a piece of thin floral wire through a piece of lace, gathering it, and attach it to the top. Add a bow and hanger, and top with globe amaranth.

FLOWER TOPIARY

Some years, December seems to be six weeks long, with enough time for everything we want to do. Other years, December has six days—max. If this is one of your short seasons, consider the advantages of an artificial tabletop tree. The base is ready-made, requiring at most a little trimming of extra-long branches. With enough natural materials, no one will ever know what it's like deep down.

This tree boasts a garland of blue larkspur glued end-to-end and spiraled down the tree. Gypsophila has been randomly scattered among the branches (a dab of hot glue on the cut stem holds each in place). Blue salvia hangs from the tips of the branches, held firmly by hot glue. Hot-glued globe amaranth blossoms cover the salvia ends and enliven other branches as well. A bow of wired ribbon tops the tree.

AVONLEA INN

Dripping with delicate icicles, draped with strings of garland, and sparkling with candlelight, this elegant inn is the quintessential Christmas house—and it's based on the real thing. With the precision of a budding architect and the artistry of a potential pastry chef, college student Kristen Cook used a turn-of-the-century inn she once

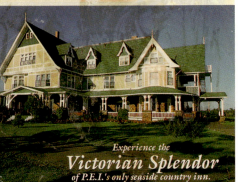

Dalvay-By-The-Sea

Experience the
Victorian Splendor
of P.E.I.'s only seaside country inn.

visited as the model for her gingerbread masterpiece. Working from a photograph, she replicated the ornate building's balconies, gables, porches, and peaks. Following is the step-by-step process she recommends for creating a gingerbread version of a real-life house of your dreams. Many of the decorating details Kristen used are described in The Trimmings, beginning on page 196.

From Real Life to Gingerbread

1. Start with a photograph of the house. If you have access to the house, take your own photographs, making sure you shoot every side and many angles, so once you start to create templates and later build, you can easily see how the "pieces" fit together. When scouting subjects, Kristen suggests, pay attention to how architecturally challenging they are. If a structure you're interested in has lots of bay windows and complicated rooflines, for example, be sure you give some thought ahead of time to the work involved in recreating those features in gingerbread. The photo on the right shows the image Kristen used as her inspiration.

2. Make a rough sketch of the four sides of your house, mainly to get an idea of how the sizes of various features will relate to one another. This process would help you determine, for example, that you want your bay windows on the front of your house to be half the size of your entrance.

3. After sketching the sides, draw a "footprint" or bird's-eye view of your structure. This sketch shows you the various roof pieces you'll need to create to replicate peaks and overhangs. The footprint also gives you an idea of the basic shape of your structure—such as whether it's an L shape or a rectangle—and shows you more about how dimensions relate to each other. Figure 1 is Kristen's footprint.

4. Using your sketches as guides, make an actual-size drawing for each side of your house, detailing each feature according to the size it will be when reproduced in gingerbread. It's best to use an architect's ruler (inexpensive and available at most hardware or office supply stores) for this step. It will allow you to make quick conversions if, for example, you want $1/4$ inch (0.6 cm) on your rough sketches to equal 1 inch (2.5 cm) on your to-scale drawings. When adding windows, doors, and other features at this stage, Kristen says she gets most of her ideas from the actual structure, but also exercises artistic freedom, sometimes adding or subtracting features and changing placement. Figure 2 shows Kristen's drawing for the left side of her inn.

5. From your to-scale drawings, create pattern pieces. Begin by studying one side at a time and determining where you have solid sections that can be single pieces of

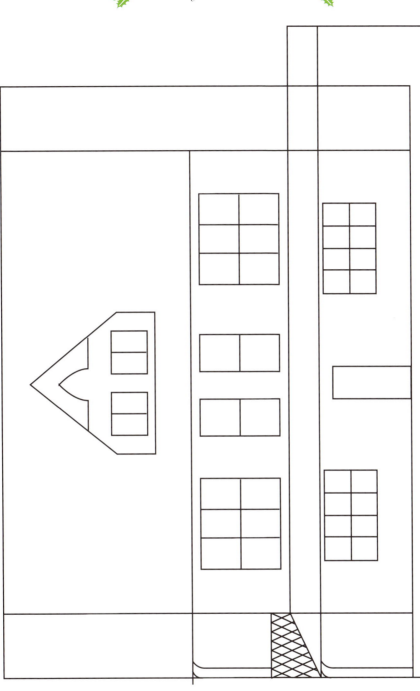

FIGURE 1

Tip: *Gingerbread is not always consistent. Learn to work with imperfections and make them part of the creative process.*

—Kristen Cook

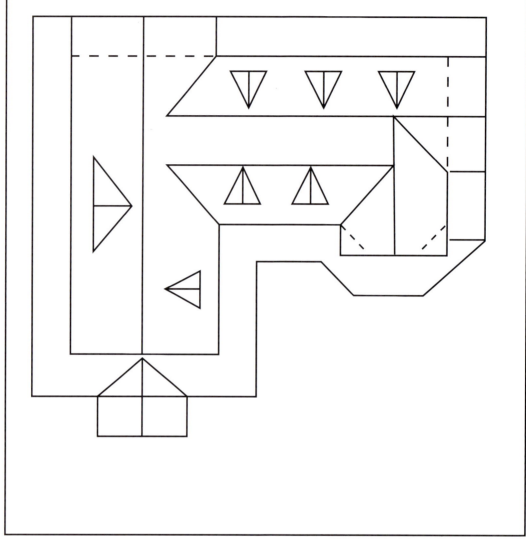

FIGURE 2

Tip: *The trick with a house this intricate is support, support, support. Kristen made double roofs everywhere she could, reproducing the small roof over the entrance and icing it in under all of her larger roofs. Flat areas always need extra support, too, so she added a duplicate layer of gingerbread under her widow's walk and other similar spots.*

gingerbread. Once you have pattern pieces for the basic structure of the house, move on to other pieces, such as porches, overhangs, window dormers, and other projections. Measure and cut out doors, windows, and any other openings you plan to create. For details on making pattern pieces, see page 186.

Kristen echoes the advice of nearly every designer featured in this book: Create pattern pieces for your entire house—and make sure they fit together as planned—before you attempt to create your house out of gingerbread. That's especially critical for a structure as detailed as this one. In fact,

Kristen baked and assembled the walls of her house first, then experimented with various pattern pieces for her multipeak roof design before settling on the ones she used.

Gingerbread Genealogy

Gingerbread has been around since early Christian times, when ancient Romans baked it in portable ovens. As early as the 1500s, inventive bakers began using it as a decorative building material. The fragrant pastry became popular in early American cooking because it was inexpensive to make—and because it could survive the unpredicta- bility of wood- and coal-fired ovens.

CANDLELIT COTTAGE

There's more than one way to make your gingerbread house glow. Using color flow (described in detail on page 200) can produce shiny, bright windows like the ones on this cozy cottage. Once the windows are completely dry, you can pipe candles and other decorations on their surface. You can use the same technique for scalloped roof pieces over your windows, or you can fashion them out of pastillage or gingerbread.

Tip: Making a gingerbread house is like getting a new dollhouse every year. I try to create houses that make people want to go inside.

—*Trish McCallister*

COVENTRY ALLEY

1. Flipping the traditional gingerbread layout shifts everyone's focus. Those who feast their eyes on this display can take a visual walk down a turn-of-the-century lane and into the heart of the hamlet. Placing the buildings on the perimeter leaves you with lots of shop window space inside to fill with everything from baskets of fresh-baked bread (peanuts are the perfect thing for these little loaves) to fruit roll-up curtains and tiny hats of piped icing.

2. If your project is heavy on architectural detail, consider creating two sets of templates. That way, you can leave the model you create for your trial run intact, and use your other set for cutting out your gingerbread pieces. When it's time to assemble the real thing, the model serves as a great guide.

3. Dried spaghetti creates the effect of window panes without obscuring the view of the scenery you fussed over inside.

4. Don't be afraid to leave well enough alone if you're creating a display with this much detail. Alex Russell, for example, said he made everything from street lamps to benches to add to his village setting, but decided not to use them because they blocked visitors' views of all the goodies inside his shops.

Tip: *Plan the size of your project so that it's something you can reasonably complete—with time and energy left over for adding lots of details.*

—Alex Russell

CHRISTMAS CHEER

This recipe makes 30 glasses of cheer on a chilly winter's day.

4 bottles red wine
16 oz/48 cL water
6 oz/18 cL dark rum
1 lemon
12 cloves
1/2 teaspoon ground cinnamon

Stick cloves into the lemon and bake in the oven for 15 minutes at 350°F/180° C. Heat the wine, water, and rum. Add the cinnamon and a little grated nutmeg to the wine mixture. Float the lemon on top. Serve in heatproof toddy glasses.

HOT EGGNOG

This is a traditional Christmas morning drink. Its origins are unclear. The name could date from the 17th Century English habit of adding a beaten egg to a small mug of strong beer—called a "noggin."

1 oz/3 cL brandy
1 oz/3 cL rum
1 free-range egg
1 teaspoon superfine (caster) sugar
hot milk

Pour all ingredients, except milk, into a highball. Top up with hot milk. Stir. Grate nutmeg over the drink.

MULLED WINE

SERVES 8

This is best made just a few hours before you want to serve it. Always use a quality dry red wine as a base for this delicious soul-warmer.

1 bottle dry red wine
1 2/3 oz/5 cL brandy
1 2/3 oz/5 cL Grand Marnier
2 teaspoons superfine (caster) sugar
3 teaspoons clear honey
2 oz/6 cL fresh orange juice
2 oz/6 cL fresh lemon juice
1 cinnamon stick
few cloves
few star anise
2 bay leaves

Put the spices together in a small cheesecloth spice bag. Place in a saucepan with the red wine, brandy, and Grand Marnier. Add the sugar and honey. Stir until both are dissolved. Add the juices. Simmer for 1 1/2 hours, stirring from time to time. Serve in a heatproof wine glass. Garnish with a slice of lemon with cloves pressed into the peel.

Chapter Three

COUNTRY CHRISTMAS

• • • • • • • • • • • •

Enjoy a rustic-inspired Christmas holiday with all the trimmings of nature. From a festive basket of pinecones to handmade place mats to lovely fir wreaths, your Christmas will reflect the simplicity of nature and home-spun traditions. Let the "country" decorating style influence your Christmas trimmings; for example, adorn a staircase with nostalgic bags full of berries and greenery, or decorate an old sled with a ribbon wreath. Create delightful outdoor scenes with the Covered Bridge Mill gingerbread house or the Snow-Covered Cottage. Bring the outdoors into your kitchen with Herbed Cheese Balls, Smoked Trout Pâté, and a Snack Basket of nuts and other goodies, which make wonderful gifts. These pages will prompt you to use nature and what you already have to create a Christmas celebration filled with pastoral crafts, decorations, and down-to-earth goodness.

SLEIGHS

The toys and goodies in these sleighs are all natural materials, wired into the spray-painted wicker sides. The white sleigh contains sprigs of holly and evergreen, peppers, cinnamon sticks, nuts, Christmas cherry, and prickly brown burrs. Riding in the red sleigh are sprigs of evergreen, statice, strawflower, peppers, cinnamon sticks, nuts, and Christmas cherry.

PINECONE FIRE STARTERS

Nothing warms the heart (and the feet) like a roaring fire, and these pinecones will set even the stubbornest logs ablaze. A perfect gift for friends with fireplaces.

Materials

Newspaper
Waxed paper
2 pounds (0.9 kg) paraffin
3 red crayons or red candle tint (or other colors)
1 teaspoon cinnamon oil (optional)
Pinecones
Basket
Ribbon
Evergreens

Tools

Double boiler or coffee can
Tongs

1. Cover your work area completely with newspaper, then with a layer of waxed paper.

2. Break the paraffin into chunks and melt it over hot water in a double boiler. Alternatively, put the wax in a clean coffee can and set it in a pan of hot water.

Caution: Paraffin is extremely flammable. Never heat it over an open flame or directly over any heat source. It may catch fire if you do. Never leave heating paraffin unattended.

3. Add crayons or candle tint (peel the paper label off the crayon first) until you're pleased with the color. Add the cinnamon oil.

4. Remove the paraffin from the heat. Using tongs, dip a pinecone into the paraffin for a few seconds. Gently lift it out without shaking off any excess wax. Allow the cone to cool for a few seconds, then set it on the waxed paper. Repeat with remaining cones.

5. After the cones are completely cool, dip them again. For second and subsequent dippings, keep the paraffin as cool as possible while keeping it liquid. Too-hot wax will melt off the residue from previous dippings.

6. Dip the cones as often as you want, until the wax is as thick as you want.

7. Arrange the cones in a basket along with a few sprigs of evergreens. Add a ribbon to the handle.

8. At the risk of sounding like an edgy aunt, caution the recipient not to store the coated cones too close to the fireplace. They really are fire starters—inside or outside the fireplace.

Shopping Tips: Paraffin: hardware stores and wherever home canning supplies are sold. Candle tints: craft stores that carry candlemaking supplies. Cinnamon oil: craft stores.

PLACE MATS
WITH DECORATIVE STITCHING

Pre-quilted fabric is available in just about any fabric store. Stitch along the convenient lines in a contrasting color to make a set of distinctive place mats.

Materials

For four place mats:
⅔ yard (61 cm) of 45-inch (114.5 cm)
pre-quilted fabric in a solid color

⅔ yard of 45-inch plain fabric (if your pre-quilted fabric is not finished on the back)
3 yards (2.8 m) of wide, double-fold bias tape
Regular sewing thread to match fabric
Heavyweight decorative rayon thread

Tools

Pencil
Sewing machine
Bobbin designed to accommodate heavy thread

1. Cut four pieces of quilted fabric 13 inches by 18 inches (33 x 45.5 cm). If the quilted fabric is not reversible, also cut four pieces of plain fabric the same size.

2. Bias binding will be easier to attach if the corners of the place mats are somewhat rounded. Draw rounded edges on the mats and cut along these lines, trying hard to make the mats symmetrical. (The safest approach is to draw a paper template and lay it over each mat before you cut.)

3. You'll be stitching with the decorative thread in the bobbin and with the material right side down. Loosen the bobbin tension on your sewing machine to compensate for the heavy decorative thread. Wind a bobbin with each color you plan to use.

4. Beginning at one edge of the place mat, stitch along the quilted lines all the way to the other edge. Cover as many lines as you like, then switch to another color.

5. Readjust the bobbin back to its normal tension and insert a bobbin with regular sewing thread. Pair up each quilted mat with a plain piece, wrong sides together. Baste around them ¼ inch (6 mm) from the edge.

6. Trim all thread ends. Fold the bias binding over the edge of the place mat, with the narrower half on the right side of the mat. Encircle each mat with bias binding and topstitch in place close to the unfolded edge. As you near your starting place, cut the tape, leaving a 1-inch (2.5 cm) overlap. Fold this end under and continue stitching.

7. If desired, stitch a decorative border on the bias tape edging.

WHITE PINE WREATH

Short branches of white pine intermingled with bunches of boxwood make a lush wreath, especially when mounted onto a thick straw base. Attach small clusters of each green onto picks, and arrange the clusters in a spiral pattern around the base. Using silver paint, spray a half-dozen magnolia pods and several branches of alder cones. Then pick them into appropriate locations around the wreath. Rather than making a conventional bow, form individual loops of silver metallic ribbon, wire them to picks, and attach each one deeply into the greenery for a contemporary look.

87

GREENERY WREATH WITH RIBBON

The natural tendency when making a wreath is to cover the entire surface of the base with decorative materials. But sometimes it's nice to add an attractive arrangement to one area, leaving the remainder unadorned as in this asymmetrical Christmas wreath. It was made on an artificial greenery base by first wiring on a bow of tapestry ribbon with additional streamers of ribbon cut and wired into the branches. Individual florets of silk hydrangea were picked and hot-glued in along with several dried lilies. Finally, silk copperberries, dried caspia, and a few gold twigs were hot-glued in.

88

FRASER FIR WREATH

Sprigs of Fraser fir define the outside of this wreath, with bright green ground pine circling the center. White yarrow and pearly everlasting, reddish brown chamaecyparis, sweet Annie, and blue-green oregano provide colorful accents. All materials are picked into a straw base.

PINE AND BABY'S BREATH SWAG

The materials for this festive garland are as simple as the technique used to make it. A length of green jute cord (the type used in macramé) was stretched taut between two chair backs, at a comfortable working height. Then bunches of pine and gypsophila (baby's breath) were alternately tied to the cord with flexible, spool-type floral wire, each bunch overlapping the previous one. Bright plaid bows were wired to the ends.

DECORATE YOUR HOME FOR A COUNTRY CHRISTMAS

❧ Diverge from the traditional fir wreath and instead decorate your door with a grand eucalyptus wreath (spray painted red) with a light pink flowers and matching bow.

❧ Adorn a staircase with nostalgic gift bags filled with greenery, pinecones, and fruit, and painted gold holly berries and leaves. The color of the bags and the greenery give a festive contrast to an oak staircase. To keep the bags from tipping over, place a rock or brick in the bottom. They can be displayed on shelves as well as stairs.

❧ A gingerbread country cottage with jelly bean "stones" and a "thatched" graham cracker roof makes an attractive display in either the dining room with all the other edibles or in the living room surrounded by books, near a fire.

❧ Transform old prints into works of art or decorate your favorite family portraits for the holidays. Simply stretch desired fabric over cardboard cut to fit inside a large frame. Staple or tape to back. Mount smaller frames inside. Hang a pine and berry spray over picture for a complete ensemble.

❧ No object should go ignored. An old wheelbarrow becomes a cheerful planter. A battered sled becomes the perfect place to hang a ribbon wreath.

❧ Transform faded paper poinsettias with a generous coat of gold glitter. The lights from the tree make them sparkle like new.

❧ Red plaid place mats and napkins make a country kitchen even cozier and all set for Christmas.

❧ Trim the tree with "ornaments" from the outside. Silver dollars, baby's breath, and red apples bring the outside in and festively incorporate the colors of the season.

❧ Crepe paper flowers transform a boring trunk into a delightful winter garden, complete with snow and tin foil icicles that shimmer against soft, white lights.

COVERED BRIDGE MILL

A single, distinctive feature can set your gingerbread display apart and provide the inspiration for even more decoration and detail. In this case, a colorful covered bridge brings the surrounding millstream setting to life. It crosses a stretch of poured sugar water, complete with rock candy river rocks.

Covered Bridge

Cut and bake your gingerbread pieces according to the templates on page 186. To color your gingerbread before baking it, add several drops of liquid food coloring to a paper cup of water. Use a pastry brush to

apply the colored water to the dough. Be sure not to add too much, or the water will run off the sides of the dough and cause the baked gingerbread to curl on the ends (creating problems when you attempt to line up pieces evenly). As your dough bakes, the color will deepen.

When your baked pieces are ready, use royal icing to assemble them according to the following instructions.

1. Start with one of the side pieces of the bridge. Pipe icing along the bottom edge, then place it on the edge of the bridge floor. Hold it in place several seconds until the icing begins to harden. You can also prop it in place with a temporary support.

2. Once the first side is stable, add the back piece, the second side, and the front piece, allowing each to stabilize before moving on to the next.

3. Allow the structure to dry completely before adding the roof pieces.

MOUNTAIN HIDEAWAY

Toss precision out the window if you're after the rustic look of rough-hewn timbers. Vary shape and thickness as you roll your logs, then texturize their surfaces with a knife. For a glossy finish, brush them before baking with a wash of egg mixed with milk or water (just be aware that this might slightly deter your gingerbread from hardening as much as it would without it). Finally, enhance the homespun look by painting your color detail directly onto the gingerbread, using a paintbrush dipped in food coloring.

SNOW-COVERED COTTAGE

This sweet design variation has storybook appeal. It's as simple as a standard box-shaped house, but the cottage's charming angles and open facade inspire decorations of whimsy and fantasy. For the Capps family, the design also inspired snow—plenty of it—complete with snowbound revelers making the most of a recent storm.

Cut and bake your gingerbread pieces according to the templates on pages 186–188. When your baked pieces are ready, use royal icing to assemble them just as you would the house in the Gingerbread Baking and Building basics section (see page 186).

Icing thick pretzel sticks on top of a gingerbread base is a quick way for kids (and bigger builders on tight schedules) to transform a standard house into a log cabin in the country. If you want a clever way to play with indoor decor, leave the back side open, and fill your rooms with candy figures. Color coconut green for leafy-looking trees like these, and melt blue hard candies for a pond.

HERBED CHEESE

Parsley, basil, rosemary, chives—fresh herbs are handsome wrappings for the smooth cheese inside. Look in upscale supermarkets or specialty food stores for fresh herbs in midwinter.

Plain goat cheese
Fresh herbs
Sweet red pepper
Extra-virgin olive oil

1. Coarsely chop herbs and peppers and place them in small bowls.

2. Form balls of goat cheese, using a small ice cream scoop. Roll balls in coatings and chill.

3. Just before serving, drizzle with olive oil and garnish with whole stems of herbs.

SMOKED TROUT PÂTÉ

Packed in a mini loaf pan or spooned into an attractive bowl, this delicate spread is a great gift during a season of constant entertaining. Smoked salmon substitutes well for the trout.

1 envelope unflavored gelatin
1/4 cup (59 ml) cold water
1/2 cup (118 ml) boiling water
1/2 cup mayonnaise
1 tablespoon lemon juice
Zest of 1 lemon
1 tablespoon coarsely chopped red onion
2 tablespoons finely chopped fresh dill
1 smoked trout fillet
1 cup (237 ml) heavy cream

1. In a large mixing bowl, soften the gelatin in the cold water. Stir in the boiling water and whisk the mixture slowly until the gelatin dissolves. Cool to room temperature.

2. Whisk in mayonnaise, lemon juice, lemon zest, onion, and dill. Refrigerate until mixture is thickened (about 15 minutes).

3. Skin the trout fillet and break the fish into flakes. Blend the fish into the mayonnaise mixture.

4. Whip the cream until soft peaks form. Fold it into the trout mixture.

5. Spoon the pâté into a mold. Refrigerate at least 4 hours.

6. Tell the recipient that the pâté can be unmolded onto a serving plate, if desired.

Yield: 2 or 3 small bread pans.

Last-Minute Version

1 pound (0.45 kg) cream cheese
⅓ cup (80 ml) sour cream
1 smoked trout fillet
1 tablespoon lemon juice
Zest of 1 lemon
2 tablespoons fresh dill

1. Skin the fillet.

2. Place all ingredients in a food processor. Mix by pulsing three or four times. (Do not overmix.) Spoon the mixture into a mold or a pretty bowl. (This version can't be unmolded.) Garnish, chill for at least 1 hour, and give away.

Yield: 2 small bread pans.

Shopping Tips: *Most well-stocked groceries carry fresh dill in the produce section. Unfortunately, dried dill just doesn't work well in this recipe.*

SNACK BASKET

Include a healthful item or two among these sweet and savory snacks, just to allay those seasonal pangs of guilt.

Materials

Yogurt-covered malt balls, pistachios, oriental rice snacks, salted almonds, mixed dried fruit, mini-pretzels, honey-roasted peanuts, or other snacks
Small brown paper bags
Flat basket
Ribbon
Pinecones
Gold spray paint (optional)

1. Weave a festive ribbon around the basket.

2. Fold over the tops of the paper bags and fill each one with a different snack.

3. Place the bags in the basket. If desired, add a few plain or gilded pinecones.

Baltimore Eggnog

In Baltimore, it was traditional for young men to call upon their friends on New Year's Day. At each of the many homes they were offered a cup of eggnog and thus they became more and more inebriated!

1 oz / 3 cL brandy
1 oz / 3 cL Madeira
2/3 oz / 2 cL dark rum
1 1/3 oz / 4 cL gomme syrup
1 free-range egg, beaten
2/3 oz / 2 cL heavy (double) cream
3 oz / 9 cL milk

Pour all ingredients into a shaker filled with ice. Shake. Strain into a highball filled with ice. Grate fresh nutmeg over the top.

For a larger crowd, make Baltimore Eggnog this way:

SERVES 10 TO 12

10 free-range eggs, beaten
5 oz / 15 cL brandy
5 oz / 15 cL Madeira
5 oz / 15 cL dark rum
13 1/3 oz / 40 cL gomme syrup
12 oz / 42 cL heavy (double) cream
12 oz / 42 cL milk

Separate the eggs. Beat the egg yolks until light. In a separate bowl, beat the egg whites until stiff. Slowly pour the brandy, Madeira, milk, and dark rum into a bunch bowl. Add the beaten yolks and egg whites. Add the gomme syrup. Whip the cream and

fold it into the mixture. Repeated folding and standing helps ripen an eggnog.

Ciderific

A terrific, simple cider-based drink to lift your spirits. The cinnamon adds a spicy finish.

2 oz / 6 cL golden rum
4 oz / 12 cL cider
stick cinnamon

Heat all ingredients in a saucepan and stir. Serve in a heatproof toddy glass. Add a few slices of apple in each drink.

Buttered Applejack

SERVES 4

A comforting cocktail for a cold winter's night.

quart / liter clear apple juice
1 oz / 3 cL fresh lemon juice
1 teaspoon grated nutmeg
1 teaspoon cinnamon
4 slices fresh gingerroot
2 teaspoons grated orange zest
1 teaspoon clear honey
1 tablespoon butter

Combine all ingredients in saucepan and heat slowly. Do not boil. When hot, use a ladle to fill four individual heatproof toddy glasses. Garnish with a cinnamon stick to use as a stirrer.

MIDNIGHT SNOWSTORM

A combination of chocolate and mint flavors all wrapped up in a creamy concoction.

1 2/3 oz / 5 cL white crème de menthe
hot chocolate
whipped cream

Pour the crème de menthe into a heatproof toddy glass. Top up with hot chocolate and float the whipped cream over the top.

SNOW BUNNY

A delectable orange and chocolate flavor comes to the fore as you stir this.

1 2/3 oz / 5 cL Grand Marnier
hot chocolate
cinnamon stick

Pour the Grand Marnier into a heatproof toddy glass. Add the hot chocolate. Stir with a cinnamon stick for the full flavor.

CINNAMON WARMER

Multiply the recipe by the number of people if you make this for a few friends.

1 1/4 oz / 3.5 cL calvados
1/2 oz / 1.5 cL dark rum
3 1/3 oz / 10 cL clear apple juice
2/3 oz / 2 cL fresh lemon juice
3 thin slices fresh gingerroot
1 teaspoon clear honey
3 cloves
1 cinnamon stick
lemon and orange peels

Pour all ingredients, except the spices, into a saucepan and heat slowly. Place the spices in a muslin cloth, tie the top in a knot, and place spices in the saucepan. Float a few twists of lemon and orange rind in the mixture. When warm, not boiled, pour into a heatproof glass.

Chapter Four

SOUTHWESTERN CHRISTMAS

• • • • • • • • • • • • •

For a fun, casual twist on your holiday celebration, consider bringing a little Southwestern flair into your home. Try the easy and fun projects, such as creating a Santa Star Pillow or trimming your packages with Cotton Seed Wraps. Or indulge your fondness for cowboys with cowboy Santa Claus ornaments and a wreath made from an old lasso. To keep the Christmas spirit alive but at the same time making great use of distinctive Southwestern materials, you can craft wreaths and ornaments out of dried chili peppers, corn husks, or even cotton seeds and shells. Try serving Red and Green Salsa as a festive way to incorporate the Southwest into your Christmas menu and are a wonderful alternative to the abundant array of sweets. The Cowboy- and Southwestern-inspired ideas in this chapter are guaranteed to bring a smile to you and your guests' faces and are a delightful variation to the traditional Christmas cheer.

SANTA STAR PILLOW

Santa has the starring role in this holiday pillow designed by Vicki Gadberry. It's a perfect weekend project for using up some of your accumulated fabric scraps, and the piecework is simple enough even for beginning sewers.

Materials & Tools

Scrap pieces of holiday fabrics
Scraps of white and black felt
Paper-backed fusible web (optional)
Sewing thread
Sewing machine
Iron
Fabric paints

Fabric glue
14" (35.6 cm) square pillow form
Stain-resisting spray

Instructions

1. Cut the fabric pieces as indicated in figure 1; the two D pieces overlap on the back to make the pillow cover function as a sham.

2. Enlarge the star pattern to fit the finished size of the center panel, piece C. Cut the star to size if you plan to attach it with fusible web. If you plan to sew the star to the pillow cover, add a seam allowance of

¼" (6 mm) all around. Attach the star to the center panel using your preferred method. Turn under and press the seam allowance before stitching.

3. Create the embellishments you desire for your Santa. In this pillow, an egg-shaped piece of white felt is used for Santa's hair and beard, and small pieces of black felt are made into boots and a belt. Cut a hole in the hair/beard to reveal a face painted onto a scrap of white cotton. His suspenders, hat, and bag are all made from holiday prints. Glue the embellishments in place, allowing each to dry before adding the next.

If desired, use a puff-type fabric paint to add fur trim to Santa's hat and suit.

4. Assemble the pieces of the front of the pillow in strips, creating two A/B/A pieces and one B/C/B segment. Now join the A/B/A pieces to the B/C/B piece. Sew all of the pieces together using a ½" (1.3 cm) seam.

5. Hem both D pieces for the back. Along one 16" (40.6 cm) edge of each piece, fold under ½" (1.3 cm) and press. Fold under another 1" (2.5 cm), press, and sew.

6. With right sides together, pin the front panel to both D pieces. The two D pieces should overlap. Sew a ½" (1.3 cm) seam on all four edges and trim the corners.

7. Turn the pillow cover right side out, pushing the corners into points. Press; then insert the pillow form. If desired, apply a stain-resisting spray to the pillow cover.

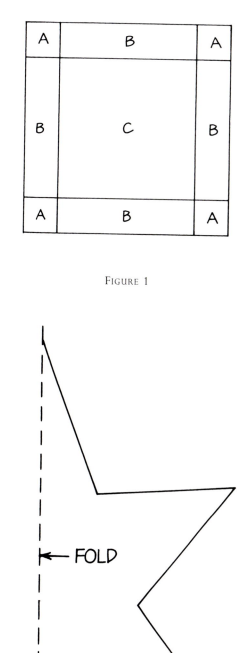

FIGURE 1

FIGURE 2

COTTON SEED WRAPS

The deep green paper is a perfect backdrop for pale flowers and dark cones. Hot-glued to the paper in a crescent shape are pinecones, cone flowers (made by cutting the cones in half), German statice, pearly everlasting, and white strawflowers. One cone is lightly dusted with white spray paint.

114

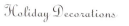
CHILI PEPPER WREATH

The scents of this herbal wreath linger in the air without overpowering all who come near. Small bunches of dried sage, mint, southernwood, and silver king artemisia were wired together, then pinned around a straw base with floral pins, with the bunches overlapping to cover the base. Accents of red peppers, globe amaranth, bittersweet berries, and yarrow were pinned among the herbs. Some of the yarrow was left its natural yellow; other was dyed a soft orange with fabric dye.

COTTON WREATH

If you mean to have a cotton-picking Christmas, here's the way to start. Mist a grapevine wreath with flat white paint from a spray can. Then wrap the wreath with narrow gold-metallic ribbon, and attach a few branches of cedar and a gold bow with hot glue. While the glue gun is still hot, attach the cotton bolls—full ones, half-open ones, and empty ones (those brown, starlike shapes). Then glue on a few sumac heads for extra color.

CORN HUSK AND STRAW WREATH

Corn husk flowers, German statice, and red velvet ribbon make a memorable wreath. First attach the flowers by twisting their wire stems around the vine base. If necessary, secure them with additional wire. The flowers should be just touching; they can be gently pulled apart later to accommodate a bow. Next, make nine or 10 bows, tuck them around the flowers, and wire them to the base. Continue to add bows until the wreath looks full enough. Hot-glue a piece of ribbon to the wreath and wrap it around the base. Finally, hot-glue pieces of German statice among the bows and down the base.

DECORATE YOUR HOME FOR A SOUTHWESTERN CHRISTMAS

❧ For a Cowboy Christmas, hang your rope on the wall and decorate with dried flowers from around the ranch tied with a cheerful bow. Accentuate with a cowboy boot ornament from the tree.

❧ For a festive centerpiece, fill a platter with candles, pinecones, and ornaments from the tree to carry your cowboy theme from the Christmas tree to the Christmas table. The ice skates symbolize unfulfilled hopes for a White Christmas.

❧ For a twist on traditional Christmas garlands, use hand-painted wooden Cowboy Santa, star, and Christmas tree ornaments, accented with bits of bandana and jute bows.

❧ Ropin' Cowboy Kringle adds a fun Southwestern feel to the traditional Santa Claus. Easily created from pine board, acrylic paint, and wire, this clever decoration brightens any spot.

❧ Make the most of all spaces. At the bottom of a wide stairway, place an old trunk and display more holiday decor, like empty packages wrapped with fabric and tie it with traditional ribbon or strips of contrasting fabric.

❧ It's the little touches that make the biggest difference. Cover tissue boxes with holiday fabric, sewn to fit standard tissue boxes and gathered at the top, tying it shut.

❧ For an easy contrast to Cowboy Santa ornaments, wrap Styrofoam balls with torn strips of bandanas and then tie like packages with jute bows.

❧ Since cowboys are known to bury their old, beloved boots, you can festively display your retired boots by filling them with holiday greenery.

WHEAT SWAG

Many craft stores carry wheat sheaves that are wired, fumigated, and ready for decorating. If you gather wheat from the fields, zap it for a few seconds in the microwave or fumigate it, to get rid of bugs. Then shape it into a sheaf and wire it together around the middle. Trim off some of the wheat heads on one side, so that the swag will hang flat against the wall. (Save the trimmings.) Make six bows with three loops on each side (you don't need a center loop), wire each in the center, and wire the bows tightly to the sheaf. Hot-glue the trimmed wheat heads randomly among the ribbons. If you hang your sheaf outside, like the one in the photo on the left, prepare to fend off hungry birds.

DRIED PEPPER ORNAMENTS

Sweet or hot, red peppers are colorful enough to hang on the tree. The large ancho peppers are tied by their stems with bright red raffia and decked out in nuts, cones, and eucalyptus—all hot-glued in place. Bright raffia bows add pizzazz.

129

The small rings were made by threading fruit and nuts onto a piece of medium-gauge floral wire, then forming the wire into a circle and hooking the ends around each other, so that the circle stays closed. The upper ornament holds nuts, hot peppers, and Christmas cherries. The lower one adds two orange calendula blossoms.

COTTON SEED ORNAMENTS

Star-shaped cotton bolls can be decorated as rustic-looking ornaments. The top one has a seed "daisy" with a gumball center and petals made from cherry pits and pumpkin seeds. The bottom boll is dressed with a small gumball and hemlock cones. Both hang from red velvet ribbons hot-glued in place.

131

TOTEM POLE LODGE

It's hard to imagine a more adventurous example of the fact that gingerbread is not just for candy Christmas cottages anymore. With tinted fondant passing for birch bark, licorice straps standing in for leather ties, and slivered almonds imitating chopped wooden accents, Tenley Rae Alaimo breaks with tradition in bright, bold style. You can build this most basic of box-shaped houses by adapting the standard house design illustrated on pages 186–188. Creating the scene is all decorating fun—adding totems and other touches in the most vivid colors and candies you can get your hands on.

Use fondant (see page 206) to make strips of birch bark for decorating your base. For appealing variation, color several different batches of fondant, creating bark ranging in shade from tan to deep brown. Then roll pieces of fondant out by hand until you have thin strips to work with (or run your fondant through a pasta machine, which makes this process even easier). If you want the crude look of natural bark, resist the temptation to use a knife to even up all the edges of your rolled fondant.

Before icing them into place, use a craft drill with a small bit to create holes in the fondant pieces where you plan to run straps of licorice. Attach the fondant to the base, allow it to dry until it's secure, then whip-stitch the licorice into place.

A wide, flat roof like this one can sag if it isn't supported well from inside. One easy and effective way to provide that support is to buy a loaf of inexpensive white bread and allow it to sit out for several days, until it takes on rock-hard form. You can then whittle the stale bread into the shapes you need and stack the pieces like a thick deck of cards inside your structure, gluing each layer together with royal icing.

TRADITIONAL LOG HOME

When you're building with gingerbread, sometimes it makes sense to draw on the same techniques you'd use if you were constructing the real thing. Pam Johnson borrowed some expertise from her husband (who builds log homes for a living) to create this mountain retreat, using a butt-and-pass log pattern mortared over a gingerbread frame. Cut your logs out of rolled sheets of gingerbread when the dough is cold, and be sure to use precise measurements if you'll be piecing them together in a pattern. When you mortar them in place, spread the icing on separately for each log; it dries too quickly to allow you to ice a whole panel at once. Use sticks of gum cut into thirds and rubbed with food coloring to create a cedar shake roof.

JERKED SPICE BLEND

Originally a Jamaican concoction, "jerked" meats have become downright trendy. This hot and spicy seasoning also jazzes up chicken, fish, and vegetables.

Ingredients

1 tablespoon onion flakes
1 tablespoon onion powder
1 tablespoon granulated garlic
2 teaspoons ground thyme
2 teaspoons salt
1 teaspoon ground allspice
¼ teaspoon ground cinnamon
¼ teaspoon ground nutmeg
2 teaspoons sugar
1 teaspoon coarsely ground black pepper
1 teaspoon cayenne pepper
2 teaspoons dried chives or green onions
Dried parsley

1. Layer the spices in a glass jar, alternating colors as desired.

2. Accompany the jar blend with the following directions: "Stir the spices well before using. Coat meat, chicken, or fish before roasting or grilling. For a flavorful dip for vegetables, mix to taste with yogurt or sour cream."

RED AND GREEN SALSAS

Traditional Christmas colors take untraditional form in this gift basket. In a season of endless sweets, picante snacks are a welcome change. Add tomato and blue corn chips for dipping.

Salsa Roja

Since "fresh" wintertime tomatoes are often pale and wan, good quality canned plum tomatoes make a better December salsa. Use one fresh tomato for texture.

1 medium tomato
6 canned plum tomatoes
4 green onions
1 clove garlic, minced
2 jalapeño peppers
4-ounce (115 g) can chopped green chiles
1 teaspoon olive oil
1 tablespoon lime juice
Salt to taste
¼ cup (59 ml) tomato juice
¼ cup (20 g) chopped cilantro

Chop the tomatoes and green onions. Mince the garlic and jalapeños. Stir in remaining ingredients.

Yield: 1½ to 2 cups

Salsa Verde

Vary the number of peppers to suit the intended receiver. In these recipes, the red salsa is considerably hotter than the green.

12 to 14 tomatillos
1 small onion, chopped
1 clove garlic, minced
1 serrano pepper, minced
2 tablespoons vegetable oil
¼ teaspoon sugar
Salt to taste
¼ cup (20 g) chopped cilantro

Remove the brown, papery husks from the tomatillos and simmer them 5 minutes, or until easily pierced with a fork. Drain and process briefly in a blender or food processor, until you have a coarse purée. Sauté the onion, garlic, and pepper in the oil 5 to 10 minutes, or until onions are soft, and add to the purée. Stir in the sugar, salt, and cilantro.

Yield: 1½ to 2 cups

VACATION EGGNOG

SERVES 10

6 oz / 18 cL dark rum
6 oz / 18 cL bourbon
6 free-range eggs, beaten
6 oz / 175 g superfine (caster) sugar
1/2 teaspoon salt
15 oz / 45cL heavy (double) cream
15 oz / 45cL milk

Pour all ingredients into a punch bowl and stir until the sugar dissolves. Place in the refrigerator for four hours. Take out of refrigerator and stir again. Serve in wine glasses. Grate fresh nutmeg over the top of each glass.

BLUE BLAZER

This drink was created by the legendary Jerry Thomas while he was at the bar of the El Dorado in San Francisco. Thomas was a star performer with this drink. He perfected the technique of lighting the whiskey and throwing the flaming liquid between two silver tankards. This act impressed President Grant so much that he presented Thomas with a cigar.

Thomas was a man of principles—he refused to serve this drink until the thermometer fell below 50 °F / 10°C. Be careful when you attempt this drink and be sure to have a fire extinguisher handy.

1 2/3 oz / 5 cL whiskey
1 2/3 oz / 5 cL boiling water
1 barspoon superfine (caster) sugar

Heat the whiskey in a small saucepan and pour into one tankard. Put the boiling water into the other tankard. Light the whiskey and, while it is flaming, pour the two liquids from one tankard to the other four times. This may seem difficult at first, and practice is required before you perform this in front of guests. Serve sweetened with sugar. Garnish with a twist of lemon.

Chapter Five

TRADITIONAL INTERNATIONAL CHRISTMAS

• • • • • • • • •

Embrace the Christmas season's unique position as the most popular cross-culture holiday by introducing a little international flavor to your celebration. Sing some of the most well-known Christmas carols that originated in Europe and have since been translated and beloved by many. Learn how to wish your friends and family from across the globe a Merry Christmas and a Happy New Year in over forty languages. In the Germanic style, you can create a lovely Table Wreath with Candles, or you can craft a European-inspired Santa with long cloaks and walking stick out of papier-mâché. Honor Mexico with *Feliz Navidad*, an adobe-style gingerbread house. Or recreate a pictorial European setting out of gingerbread houses with the Holiday Village, the Christmas Wedding Chapel, and the Cathedral at Christmas. Indulge in a little holiday cheer with enjoyable international beverages, such as Canadian Cocoa, Italian Coffee, and *Glühwein*. Learn from other cultures and have a very, Merry Christmas and a Happy New Year, or should that be *Maligayang Pasko at Manigong Bagong Taon*!

Silent Night

(1818, W. German anonymous,
translated into English by Joseph Mohr, 1871,
melody Franz Gruber)

1.

Silent night, holy night
All is calm, all is bright
Round yon Virgin Mother and Child
Holy Infant so tender and mild
Sleep in heavenly peace
Sleep in heavenly peace

2.

Silent night, holy night
Shepherds quake at the sight
Glories stream from Heaven afar
Heav'nly hosts sing Alleluia
Christ the Saviour is born
Christ the Saviour is born

3.

Silent night, holy night
Son of God, love's pure light
Radiant beams from Thy holy face
With the dawn of redeeming grace
Jesus, Lord at thy birth
Jesus, Lord at thy birth

The First Noel

(1833)

1.

The first Nowell the angel did say
Was to certain poor shepherds in
    fields as they lay
In fields where they lay keeping
    their sheep
On a cold winter's night that
    was so deep
Nowell, Nowell, Nowell, Nowell,
Born is the King of Israel

2.

They looked up and saw a star
Shining in the East beyond them afar
And to the earth it gave great life
And so it continued both day
    and night

3.

And by the light of that same star
Three wise men came from country far
To seek the king was their intent
And to follow the star wherever it went

4.

This star drew nigh to the northwest
O'er Bethlehem it took its rest
And there it did both stop and stay
Right over the place where Jesus lay

5.

Then entered in those wise men three
Full reverently upon their knee
And offered there in his presence
Their gold and myrrh and frankincense

6.

Then let us all with one accord
Sing praises to our Heavenly Lord
That hath made Heaven and earth
    of nought
And with His blood mankind
    hath bought

The Twelve Days of Christmas

(1500s)

On the first day of Christmas,
my true love sent to me
A partridge in a pear tree.

On the second day of Christmas,
my true love sent to me
Two turtle doves
And a partridge in a pear tree.

On the third day of Christmas,
my true love sent to me
Three French hens,
Two turtle doves,
And a partridge in a pear tree.

On the fourth day of Christmas,
my true love sent to me
Four calling birds,
Three French hens,
Two turtle doves,
And a partridge in a pear tree.

On the fifth day of Christmas,
my true love sent to me
Five golden rings,
Four calling birds,
Three French hens,
Two turtle doves,
And a partridge in a pear tree.

On the sixth day of Christmas,
my true love sent to me
Six geese a-laying,
Five golden rings,
Four calling birds,
Three French hens,
Two turtle doves,
And a partridge in a pear tree.

On the seventh day of Christmas,
my true love sent to me
Seven swans a-swimming,
Six geese a-laying,
Five golden rings,
Four calling birds,
Three French hens,
Two turtle doves,
And a partridge in a pear tree.

On the eighth day of Christmas,
my true love sent to me
Eight maids a-milking,
Seven swans a-swimming,
Six geese a-laying,
Five golden rings,
Four calling birds,
Three French hens,
Two turtle doves,
And a partridge in a pear tree.

On the ninth day of Christmas,
my true love sent to me
Nine ladies dancing,
Eight maids a-milking,
Seven swans a-swimming,
Six geese a-laying,
Five golden rings,
Four calling birds,
Three French hens,
Two turtle doves,
And a partridge in a pear tree.

On the tenth day of Christmas,
my true love sent to me
Ten lords a-leaping,
Nine ladies dancing,
Eight maids a-milking,
Seven swans a-swimming,
Six geese a-laying,
Five golden rings,
Four calling birds,
Three French hens,
Two turtle doves,
And a partridge in a pear tree.

On the eleventh day of Christmas,
my true love sent to me
Eleven pipers piping,
Ten lords a-leaping,
Nine ladies dancing,
Eight maids a-milking,
Seven swans a-swimming,
Six geese a-laying,
Five golden rings,
Four calling birds,
Three French hens,
Two turtle doves,
And a partridge in a pear tree.

On the twelfth day of Christmas,
my true love sent to me
Twelve drummers drumming,
Eleven pipers piping,
Ten lords a-leaping,
Nine ladies dancing,
Eight maids a-milking,
Seven swans a-swimming,
Six geese a-laying,
Five golden rings,
Four calling birds,
Three French hens,
Two turtle doves,
And a partridge in a pear tree.

Angels We Have Heard on High

(M. MEDIEVAL, W. 1700S)

1.

Angels we have heard on high
Sweetly singing o'er the plains,
And the mountains in reply
Echoing their joyous strains.

Refrain
Gloria, in excelsis Deo!
Gloria, in excelsis Deo!

2.

Shepherds, why this jubilee?
Why your joyous strains prolong?
What the gladsome tidings be
Which inspire your heavenly song?

Refrain

3.

Come to Bethlehem and see
Christ Whose birth the angels sing;
Come, adore on bended knee,
Christ the Lord, the newborn King.

Refrain

4.

See Him in a manger laid,
Whom the choirs of angels praise;
Mary, Joseph, lend your aid,
While our hearts in love we raise.

How to Say Merry Christmas
(and Happy New Year) Around the World

(ALBANIAN) *Gezur Krislinjden*

(ARABIC) *Idah Saidan Wa Sanah Jadidah*

(ARGENTINE) *Feliz Navidad Y Un Prospero Año Nuevo*

(ARMENIAN) *Shenoraavor Nor Dari yev Pari Gaghand*

(BOHEMIAN) *Vesele Vanoce*

(BRAZILIAN) *Feliz Natal e Prospero Ano Novo*

(CHINA—CANTONESE) *Gun Tso Sun Tan'Gung Haw Sun Sing Dan Fai Lok*

(CHINA—MANDARIN) *Kung His Hsin Nien bing Chu Shen Tan Sheng Dan Kuai Le*

(CROATIAN) *Sretan Bozic Èestit Boiæ i sretna Nova godina*

(CZECH) *Prejeme Vam Vesele Vanoce a stastny Novy Rok*

(DANISH) *Gledlig jul og godt Nytt Aar*

(DUTCH) *Vrolijk; Kerstfeest en een Gelukkig Nieuwjaar; Prettig Kerstfeest*

(FINNISH) *Hauskaa Joulua Hyvää joulua ja Onnellista uutta vuotta*

(FRENCH) *Joyeux Noël et Heureuse Année*

(GAELIC-IRISH) *Nolag mhaith Dhuit Agus Bliain Nua Fe Mhaise*

(GAELIC-SCOT) *Nollaig Chridheil agus Bliadhna Mhath Ur*

(GERMAN) *Frohe Weihnachten und ein glückliches neues Jahr*

(GREEK) *Kala Khristougena kai Eftikhes to Neon Ethos*

(HAWAIIAN) *Mele Kalikimake me ka Hauloi Makahiki hou*

(HEBREW) *Mo'adim Lesimkha*

(HINDI) *Shubh Christmas*

(HUNGARIAN) *Kellemes Karacsonyi unnepeket Boldog Karacsonyl es Ujevl Unnepeket Kellemes Karacsonyt Es Boldog Uj Evet*

(ICELANDIC) *Gledileg jol og farsaelt komandi ar Gledlig jol og Nyar*

(INDONESIA) *Selamat Hari Natal / Selamah Tahun Baru*

(IRISH) *Nollaig Shona Duit, Nodlaig mhaith chugnat*

(ITALIAN) *Buon Natale e Felice Anno Nuovo Buone Feste Natalizie Buon Natale e felice Capodanno*

(JAPANESE) *Shinnen omedeto / Kurisumasu Omedeto*

(KOREAN) *Chuk Sung Tan / Sung Tan Chuk Ha.*

(LITHUANIAN) *Linksmu Kaledu linksmu sventu Kaledu ir Laimingu Nauju Metu*

(NORWEGIAN) *God Jul Og Godt Nytt Aar*

(PERUVIAN) *Feliz Navidad y un Venturoso / Año Nuevo*

(PHILIPINO) *Maligayang Pasko at Manigong Bagong Taon*

(POLISH) *Wesolych Swiat Bozego Narodzenia i szczesliwego Nowego Roku*

(PORTUGUESE) *Boas Festas e Feliz Ano Novo Feliz Natal e propero Ano Novo*

(ROMANIAN) *Sarbatori Fericite. La Multi Ani*

(RUSSIAN) *S'prazdnikom Rozdestva Hristova i s' Novim Godom*

(SERBIAN) *Hristos se rodi*

(SERBO-CROATIAN) *Sretam Bozic. Vesela Nova Godina*

(SPANISH) *Feliz Navidad y prospero Año Nuevo*

(SWEDISH) *God Jul Och Gott Nytt År*

(TURKISH) *Noeliniz Ve Yeni Yiliniz Kutlu Olsun Yeni Yilnizi Kutar, saadetler dilerim*

(UKRAINIAN) *Srozhdestvom Kristovym*

(VIETNAMESE) *Mung Le Giang Sinh / Cung Chuc Tan Nien*

(WELSH) *Nadolic Llawen / Blwyddn Newdd Dda*

NEEDLEPOINT ORNAMENTS

Noted for her use of bright colors and attention to detail, needlepoint designer Catherine Reurs added a touch of whimsy to this trio of Santas. These are quick, fun projects to frame individually, hang together on a wide ribbon, or display as Christmas tree ornaments.

Materials & Tools

clear plastic needlepoint canvas (14 mesh)
china marker, grease pencil, or felt pen
#22 tapestry needle
Paternayan Persian Tapestry Wool:

SANTA SAILING
3 yds. (2.7 m) white #260
2 yds. (1.8 m) red #970
2 yds. (1.8 m) green #680
1 yd. (91.4 cm) black #221
2 yds. (1.8 m) cobalt blue #540
1 yd. (91.4 cm) flesh #490
5 yds. (4.6 m) sky blue #544
1 yd. (91.4 cm) very pale blue #546
10 yds. (9.1 m) metallic gold

SANTA & FRIENDS
4 yds. (3.7 m) white #260
3 yds. (2.7 m) red #970
2 yds. (1.8 m) green #680
1 yd. (91.4 cm) black #221
1 yd. (91.4 cm) cobalt blue #540
1 yd. (91.4 cm) flesh #490
1 yd. (91.4 cm) very pale blue #546
2 yds. (1.8 m) golden brown #720
5 yds. (4.6 m) deep yellow #771

5 yds. (4.6 m) metallic gold
10 yds. (9.1 m) metallic red
10 yds. (9.1 m) metallic green

SANTA AT THE PYRAMIDS
1 yd. (91.4 cm) white #260
2 yds. (1.8 m) red #970
3 yds. (2.7 m) green #680
1 yd. (91.4 cm) black #221
1 yd. (91.4 cm) cobalt blue #540
1 yd. (91.4 cm) flesh #490
6 yds. (5.5 m) golden brown #720
5 yds. (4.6 m) yellow #772
5 yds. (4.6 m) light purple #341
6 yds. (5.5 m) deep purple #340
10 yds. (9.1 m) metallic red
3 yds. (2.7 m) metallic silver

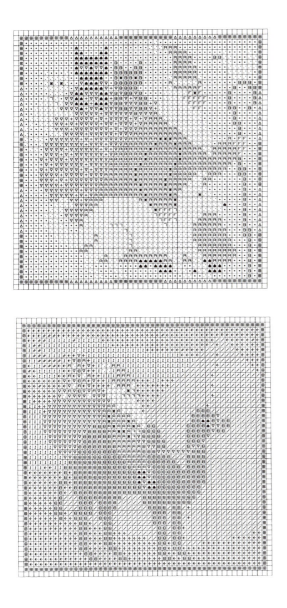

Key to Charts

	Color	Paternayan Wool
♠	= Black	#221
◢	= Metallic Silver	Silver
⅂	= Very Pale Blue	#546
∴	= White	#260
B	= Golden Brown	#720
+	= Metallic Gold	Gold
◥	= Yellow	#772
○	= Dark Yellow	#771
✳	= Cobalt Blue	#540
╱	= Sky Blue	#544
→	= Deep Purple	#340
1	= Light Purple	#341
F	= Flesh	#490
R	= Red	#970
⊞	= Metallic Red	Red
▽	= Green	#680
△	= Metallic Green	Green

1. Copy the pattern shape onto the plastic canvas before you cut the canvas to size. Mark the outline of each piece on the canvas and count the bars in each piece to check it before cutting. When cutting the

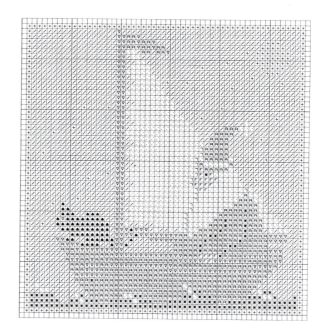

canvas, cut the space between the bars and trim off all the plastic nubs. Then clean off the outline marks.

2. Separate the 3-ply yarn into single plies and thread the needle with one ply of yarn. Work all of the designs with a single ply.

3. Referring to the charts, work the designs in the continental or basketweave stitch, starting in the center or in one corner. Stitch the design details first; then fill in the background. Finish with the outside border.

4. Needlepoint hints: Wherever possible, work the lightest colors first. This prevents you from catching any dark threads and stitching them into the lighter colors. Don't pull the stitches too tightly, or the canvas may tear. When you come to the end of a strand of wool, gently run it through

the back of 7 to 10 stitches to prevent it from working loose. Don't carry the wool from one area of color to another of the same color unless it is within five to six stitches in any direction. Leave the outside row on all sides unstitched until the rest of the piece is complete; then use a binding stitch to finish the edges.

5. Because the plastic canvas is rigid, your finished needlepoint won't need to be blocked. For ornaments, sew a ribbon loop on the back of each design and glue felt or ultrasuede on the back to finish it. To make a small wall hanging, slip stitch or glue each Santa to a wide ribbon, leaving 2" (5.1 cm) of ribbon showing between each. Add a simple bow at the top. Alternatively, frame each Santa individually and display the trio on your mantelpiece.

SANTA'S SAMPLER

Peggy Hayes designed this sampler to welcome guests of all nationalities to your home for the holidays. Use the last line to personalize your sampler with your own name (or that of the person for whom you're making it) or with your own favorite holiday greeting.

Merry Christmas

Feliz Navidad

Joyeux Noel

Frohe Weihnachten

Your Name Here

Materials & Tools

14-count Aida cloth in mushroom color
14 1/2 " x 16 1/2 " (36.8 x 41.9 cm)
tapestry needle

DMC colors (1 skein of each):
white
ecru
darkest cranberry #815
light creamy peach #754
country blue denim #930
medium country blue #932
dark pistachio #367
light honey #676
dark country blue #931
dark spruce #890
medium pistachio #320
dark honey #680
dark golden brown #434
darkest silver #317
medium pecan #840
medium silver #318
gold metallic embroidery thread

Instructions

1. Mark the horizontal and vertical center of the canvas with basting thread.

2. Using two strands of floss in your needle, cross-stitch the design according to the chart. Back-stitch (outline-stitch) the lettering in two strands of darkest silver, snowflakes in two strands of medium country blue, small border in two strands of dark golden brown, and center of the large border in one strand of gold metallic thread.

3. Using two strands of the same color floss, back-stitch around these completed designs: hat; eyes; large green, gold, and blue presents; small presents in sampler; bells in sampler; and small border. Use two strands of medium pecan to back-stitch around the fur on the hat and gloves. Back-stitch around the hair, beard, mustache, eyebrows, and face with two strands of medium silver.

4. For the ribbons on all of the presents, back-stitch in extra-long stitches with gold metallic thread. Tie a bow with gold metallic thread on the large blue present.

5. Make two French knots over the e in Noël and a single French knot under each bell. Sew a glass seed bead at the top of each Christmas tree.

6. Stretch and frame the finished needlework as desired.

Key to Chart

◣ = Dark Spruce

⋒ = Darkest Cranberry

■ = Country Blue Denim

● = Light Honey

⋒ = Dark Golden Brown

⊔ = Light Creamy Peach

⊐ = Dark Country Blue

— = Dark Honey

· = White

⊏ = Medium Pistachio

∨ = Ecru

| = Medium Country Blue

╱ = Dark Pistachio

TABLE WREATH WITH CANDLES

To make a festive table wreath that is not only beautiful to look at but has a heavenly fragrance, gather a selection of scented geraniums: peppermint, staghorn oak, and rose. Push the leaf stems into a moistened oasis ring that has been wired to maintain its shape. To create a lush, verdant setting, add trailing rosemary and lemon verbena.

The vivid red accents consist of pineapple sage (the tubular blossoms), red celosia, and a few fresh strawflowers. The deep lavender blooms are Mexican bush sage. With a trio of red candles, this wreath makes a stunning centerpiece, and if kept cool when not being used, it will still look fresh more than a week later.

WONDROUS SANTA

This saintly figure has a rapturous expression as he contemplates the night sky and his long journey ahead. Designer Christi Hensley achieves this glow by dipping the painted papier-mâché face into a bath of melted wax.

Materials & Tools

Aluminum foil

Instant papier-mâché

Sandpaper

Gesso sealer

Acrylic paints

Artist's brushes

2 lbs. (908 g) candle wax

Coffee can

Lamb's wool

Poster board

Glue gun

½ yd. (45.7 cm) fabric for undergarment

1½ yd. (1.4 m) upholstery fabric

½ yd. (45.7 cm) trim fabric

Sewing machine and thread (optional)

Polyester fiberfill

Strong rubber band

Scrap of black fabric

½ yd. (45.7 cm) burlap

23" (58.4 cm) stick

Pinecones and berries

Decorative cord with tassel

1. Form a 3" (7.6 cm) ball of aluminum foil, leaving a neck stem about ½" (1.3 cm) wide and 1½" (3.8 cm) long (figure 1).

2. Mix the instant papier-mâché according to the manufacturer's directions and apply a coating about ¼" (6 mm) thick over the aluminum base. After the initial layer has dried, model the nose, cheeks, and mouth. Creating the features may take a few layers; allow the papier-mâché to dry between applications.

3. To prepare the head for painting, smooth it with sandpaper and apply two coats of gesso. Use a skin tone as a base coat over the entire head. After this has dried, paint on the features, using the photograph as a guide.

4. Place the wax in a coffee can and heat it in a pan of hot water until it reaches a temperature of about 190°F (90°C). Holding the head by the neck, dip it into the wax as far as possible. Remove the head in one continuous movement, tilting the features up so that any excess wax drips to the back. Let the wax harden and dip again.

5. Glue won't stick to wax, so scrape the beard, hair, and eyebrow areas. Attach the wool at these points with hot glue.

6. Trim the poster board to 28" x 18" (71.1 x 45.7 cm) and form it into a cone with a 1" (2.5 cm) opening at the top and a 9" (22.9 cm) opening at the bottom. After securing it with hot glue, trim the cone so that it will stand (figure 2).

7. To cover the body of the figure, cut a piece of fabric 9" x 21" (22.9 x 53.3 cm) for the undergarment. Glue this lengthwise to the front of the cone, tucking under the edges at the top and bottom and gluing them to the inside of the cone. Cut a piece of coat fabric 21" x 40" (53.3 x 101.6 cm) and two pieces of trim fabric 6" x 21" (15.2 x 53.3 cm). Sew or glue the trim to the shorter edges of the coat. Then fold

each piece of trim in half lengthwise and hem or glue the raw edge to the inside of the coat.

8. Cut one 7" x 21" (17.8 x 53.3 cm) piece of coat fabric for the arms. Cut two pieces of trim fabric 5" x 7" (12.7 x 17.8 cm) and sew or glue these to the short edges. Then fold the trim and hem or glue it to the wrong side of the fabric. With the right sides together, fold the sleeve in half lengthwise and make a seam. Turn the right side out and lightly stuff the tube with polyester. Now mark the center; each half becomes an arm.

9. For the hood, cut a 10" (25.4 cm) right triangle of coat fabric and a strip of trim 6" x 15" (15.2 x 38.1 cm). Attach the trim to the longer edge of the triangle, turning and hemming it as before. With right sides together, fold the triangle so that the equal

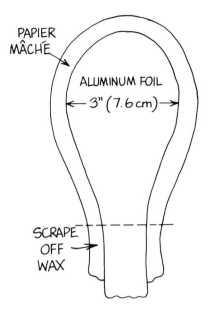

PAPIER MÂCHÉ

ALUMINUM FOIL

← 3" (7.6 cm) →

SCRAPE OFF WAX

FIGURE 1

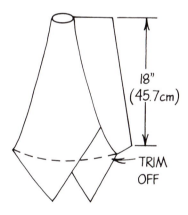

18" (45.7cm)

TRIM OFF

FIGURE 2

sides meet. Sew down 5" (12.7 cm) from the right angle corner; then turn the piece right side out.

10. Attach the coat to the body by gathering it around the cone so that the front edges are slightly open to reveal the undergarment. Secure the gathers at the top of the cone with a strong rubber band, leaving about 1" of fabric above the top of the cone. After applying glue to the inside top edge of the cone, push the excess fabric into the opening.

11. To assemble the figure, attach the center of the arm piece to the center back of the coat at arm level. Glue the head into the top of the cone and place the hood. Turn and glue the raw edges at the front of the hood so that they are disguised by the beard. Make two mittens from the black fabric, add stuffing, and attach them to the arms. Using the burlap, cut a circle of fabric for the sack. Fill it with polyester and gather the edges with a decorative ribbon. Glue the sack onto the figure's back, covering the attachment of the arms, and glue one hand to the top of the bag. Glue the other hand to a stick decorated with pinecones, berries, and such. Finally, place a decorative cord with tassel around the saint's neck.

FIR TREE TOPIARY

Flat but emphatically three-dimensional, this two-foot-tall (60 cm) wall tree supplies that indispensable Christmas tree fragrance. The base is a sheet of two-inch-thick (5 cm) plastic foam cut in a tree shape. Pieces of Fraser fir are inserted at a sharp, downward-sloping angle, to mimic tree branches. Sumac heads and sprigs of German statice, both picked into the base, provide the red and white decorations.

HOLIDAY VILLAGE

Talk about a light bulb going off. Trish McCallister started by making a simple chocolate lamppost, just to get the creative juices flowing. Before she knew it, this entire snow-swept village began springing up around her little light. A collection of constructions makes for a striking gingerbread display. Keep your shapes fairly standard, like the ones shown here. Then add your variety in the form of roofing material, window dressing, door shapes and styles, and color. Trish says her plan was to "make people want to look at all the little spaces," as if they were actually touring a gingerbread village.

FELIZ NAVIDAD

Forget the North Pole. Emily Grace Young let her imagination drift southward (Southwest, to be exact) to come up with this holiday hacienda and church. She also used a clever gingerbread alternative that's perfect for younger builders—graham crackers. You can glue them together with royal icing, just as you would pieces of gingerbread. If you want to cut out windows and doors, do that first by warming the crackers briefly in the oven to soften them up. Because graham cracker structures are quicker and easier to assemble than walls and roofs of gingerbread, they leave small chefs plenty of time and energy for decorating. Use pink-tinted royal icing to create adobe-like surfaces, and accent your buildings and yard with easy-to-find foods. The wagon here features pretzels and pasta wheels. Sugar wafer cookies form the well and the cactus. And a sprinkling of brown sugar gives a sandy sparkle to the warm-weather holiday scene.

CHRISTMAS WEDDING CHAPEL

Christmas is for lovers, according to Lisa Goelz, who studded her chapel doors with candy hearts and land- scaped the lawn with a bride, a groom, and a just-married sleigh, ready to whisk the happy couple down a red licorice drive.

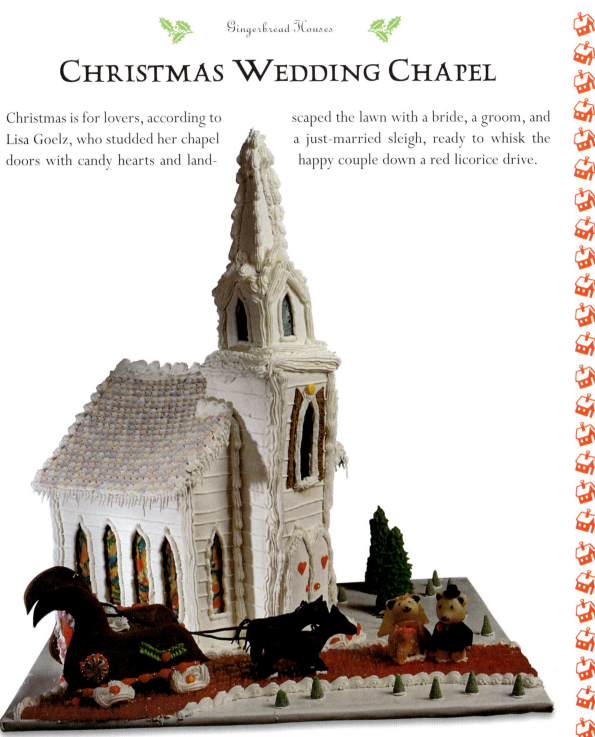

CATHEDRAL AT CHRISTMAS

Create a regal house of worship with a two-story facade and elegant arched windows, all adorned with minimal, classic touches. For frosty, amber-colored windows like these, cook poured sugar until it caramelizes.

CANADIAN COCOA

This beverage has a wonderful vanilla and chocolate milk flavor, with the additional sweetness of maple syrup.

2/3 oz / 2 cL Canadian rye whiskey
2/3 oz / 2 cL dark rum
1/2 oz / 1.5 cL white crème de cacao
dash maple syrup
hot, frothy milk

Pour all ingredients, except milk, into a heatproof toddy glass. Stir. Add the hot, frothy milk. Stir. Grate fresh nutmeg over the drink.

HOT SCOTCH TODDY

The word "toddy" might come from "tarrie," a 17th century word for a drink made from palm tree sap and drunk in the East Indies. Yet, as early as 1721 the Scottish poet Allan Ramsey made a claim that it is derived from Tod's Well, a source of Edinburgh water.

1 2/3 oz / 5 cL Scotch
2 1/3 oz / 7 cL boiling water
1/3 oz / 1 cL fresh lemon juice
3 dashes Angostura bitters
1 teaspoon clear honey
3 cloves
twist of lemon

Pour the Scotch, boiling water, lemon juice, and Angostura bitters into a heatproof toddy glass. Stir to dissolve the honey. Spear the cloves into the twist of lemon and add to the drink.

IRISH COFFEE

A soothing drink that was born at a freezing cold airfield at Shannon Airport, near Ireland's Atlantic Coast, just after the Second World War. The airport was a refueling stop for transatlantic aircraft, and while on the ground, the passengers were refueled by Irishman Joe Sheridan. He took the traditional Irish drink, whiskey in tea, and substituted coffee for tea to suit the Americans' tastes. Adding a thick whirl of lightly whipped Irish cream on top, and sugar, he served this in a stemmed glass to his customers.

The first Irish coffee was taken to San Francisco by the late writer, Stanton Delaplane, and served in 1952 at the Buena Vista bar at Fisherman's Wharf.

2 teaspoons brown sugar
1 3/4 oz / 5 cL Irish whiskey
3 1/2 oz / 10 cL hot coffee
2/3 oz / 2 cL whipped cream

Pour the whiskey into a large, heatproof, goblet. Add the brown sugar and stir. Add the hot coffee and stir with a teaspoon. Gently float the whipped cream over a barspoon to create a final layer. Do not stir. Serve while hot.

GLÜHWEIN

This is a classic German-style hot toddy. The wine is more prominent in this rich combination.

2 cubes sugar
1 slice lemon
1 cinnamon stick
8 oz / 24 cL red wine

Boil all ingredients in a saucepan and serve as hot as possible. Serve in a heatproof toddy glass.

ITALIAN COFFEE

Coffee with a wonderful nutty flavor and a layer of whipped cream tops off a fine evening.

1 oz / 3 cL amaretto
2/3 oz / 2 cL coffee liqueur
hot coffee
whipped cream

Place a barspoon in a heatproof toddy glass. Add the amaretto and coffee liqueur. Fill with coffee. Stir. Float the cream over the top. Garnish with three coffee beans.

Chapter Six

NOT-QUITE GROWN-UP CHRISTMAS

• • • • • • • • • • • •

Pass along your most-loved carols, like "Jingle Bells," and favorite stories, such as "Yes, Virginia, There Is a Santa Claus" and "The Little Match Seller" to your beloved youngsters. Or you can sing and reread them for your own pleasure as this chapter is intended for the young in body and the young in spirit! Build the beautiful tole-painted sled that you never had or that you always dreamed of giving to your child. Have fun making the most adorable Santa Hand Puppet or the very clever Somersaulting Santa. Give the traditional gingerbread house a playful twist by creating Santa's Palace, a Candy Land Christmas, or even a Merry-Go-Round. Remember, children are an essential part of Christmas, since indeed Christmas celebrates the birth of Jesus. So let your inner-child run wild as you create the best Christmas ever!

Jingle Bells

(James Pierpont, 1857)

1.

Dashing through the snow
On a one-horse open sleigh,
Over the fields we go,
Laughing all the way;
Bells on bob-tail ring,
making spirits bright,
What fun it is to ride and sing
A sleighing song tonight

Refrain:

Jingle bells, jingle bells,
jingle all the way!
O what fun it is to ride
In a one-horse open sleigh

2.

A day or two ago,
I thought I'd take a ride,
And soon Miss Fanny Bright
Was seated by my side;
The horse was lean and lank;
Misfortune seemed his lot;
He got into a drifted bank,
And we, we got upsot.

Refrain

3.

A day or two ago,
the story I must tell
I went out on the snow
And on my back I fell;
A gent was riding by
In a one-horse open sleigh,
He laughed as there I sprawling lie,
But quickly drove away.

Refrain

4.

Now the ground is white
Go it while you're young,
Take the girls tonight
And sing this sleighing song;
Just get a bob-tailed bay
two-forty as his speed
Hitch him to an open sleigh
And crack! you'll take the lead.

Refrain

Joy to the World

(1839)

1.
Joy to the world! The Lord is come:
let earth receive her King!
Let every heart prepare him room,
and heaven and nature sing.

2.
Joy to the earth! The Saviour reigns:
let men their songs employ!
while fields and floods, rocks, hills
        and plains
repeat the sounding joy.

3.
No more let sins and sorrows grow
nor thorns infest the ground:
He comes to make his blessings flow
far as the curse is found.

4.
He rules the earth with truth
        and grace,
and makes the nations prove
the glories of his righteousness
and wonders of his love.

Yes, Virginia, There is a Santa Claus

Editorial Page, *New York Sun*, 1897

We take pleasure in answering thus prominently the communication below, expressing at the same time our great gratification that its faithful author is numbered among the friends of The Sun:

I am eight years old. Some of my little friends say there is no Santa Claus. Papa says, "If you see it in The Sun, it's so." Please tell me the truth, is there a Santa Claus?
—Virginia O'Hanlon

Virginia, your little friends are wrong. They have been affected by the skepticism of a sceptical age. They do not believe except what they see. They think that nothing can be which is not comprehensible by their little minds. All minds, Virginia, whether they be men's or children's, are little. In this great universe of ours, man is a mere insect, an ant, in his intellect as compared with the boundless world about him, as measured by the intelligence capable of grasping the whole of truth and knowledge.

Yes, Virginia, there is a Santa Claus.

He exists as certainly as love and generosity and devotion exist, and you know that they abound and give to your life its highest beauty and joy. Alas! how dreary would be the world if there were no Santa Claus! It would be as dreary as if there were no Virginias. There would be no childlike faith then, no poetry, no romance to make tolerable this existence. We should have no enjoyment, except in sense and sight. The external light with which childhood fills the world would be extinguished.

Not believe in Santa Claus! You might as well not believe in fairies. You might get your papa to hire men to watch in all the chimneys on Christmas eve to catch Santa Claus, but even if you did not see Santa Claus coming down, what would that prove? Nobody sees Santa Claus, but that is no sign that there is no Santa Claus. The most real things in the world are those that neither children nor men can see. Did you ever see fairies dancing on the lawn? Of course not, but that's no proof that they are not there. Nobody can conceive or imagine all the wonders there are unseen and unseeable in the world.

You tear apart the baby's rattle and see what makes the noise inside, but there is a veil covering the unseen world which not the strongest man, nor even the united strength of all the strongest men that ever lived, could tear apart. Only faith, poetry, love, romance, can push aside that curtain and view and picture the supernal beauty and glory beyond. Is it all real? Ah, Virginia, in all this world there is nothing else real and abiding.

No Santa Claus? Thank God he lives and lives forever. A thousand years from now, Virginia, nay, 10 times 10,000 years from now, he will continue to make glad the heart of childhood.

Merry Christmas and a Happy New Year!!!!

THE LITTLE MATCH-SELLER

BY HANS CHRISTIAN ANDERSEN (1846)

'Twas terribly cold and nearly dark on the last evening of the old year, and the snow was falling fast. In the cold and the darkness, a poor little girl, with bare head and naked feet, roamed through the streets. It is true she had on a pair of slippers when she left home, but they were not of much use. They were very large, so large, indeed, that they had belonged to her mother, and the poor little creature had lost them in running across the street to avoid two carriages that were rolling along at a terrible rate. One of the slippers she could not find, and a boy seized upon the other and ran away with it, saying that he could use it as a cradle, when he had children of his own. So the little girl went on with her little naked feet, which were quite red and blue with the cold. In an old apron she carried a number of matches, and had a bundle of them in her hands. No one had bought anything of her the whole day, nor had anyone given her even a penny. Shivering with cold and hunger, she crept along; poor little child, she looked the picture of misery. The snowflakes fell on her long, fair hair, which hung in curls on her shoulders, but she regarded them not.

Lights were shining from every window,

and there was a savory smell of roast goose, for it was New-year's eve—yes, she remembered that. In a corner, between two houses, one of which projected beyond the other, she sank down and huddled herself together. She had drawn her little feet under her, but she could not keep off the cold; and she dared not go home, for she had sold no matches, and could not take home even a penny of money. Her father would certainly beat her; besides, it was almost as cold at home as here, for they had only the roof to cover them, through which the wind howled, although the largest holes had been stopped up with straw and rags. Her little hands were almost frozen with the cold. Ah! perhaps a burning match might be some good, if she could draw it from the bundle and strike it against the wall, just to warm her fingers. She drew one out—"scratch!" how it sputtered as it burnt! It gave a warm, bright light, like a little candle, as she held her hand over it. It was really a wonderful light. It seemed to the little girl that she was sitting by a large iron stove, with polished brass feet and a brass ornament. How the fire burned! and seemed so beautifully warm that the child stretched out her feet as if to warm them, when, lo! the flame of the match went out, the stove vanished, and she had only the remains of the half-burnt match in her hand.

She rubbed another match on the wall. It burst into a flame, and where its light fell upon the wall it became as transparent as a veil, and she could see into the room. The table was covered with a snowy white tablecloth, on which stood a splendid dinner service, and a steaming roast goose, stuffed with apples and dried plums. And what was still more wonderful, the goose jumped down from the dish and waddled across the floor, with a knife and fork in its breast, to the little girl. Then the match went out, and there remained nothing but the thick, damp, cold wall before her.

She lighted another match, and then she found herself sitting under a beautiful Christmas tree. It was larger and more beautifully decorated than the one which she had seen through the glass door at the rich merchant's. Thousands of tapers were burning upon the green branches, and colored pictures, like those she had seen in the showwindows, looked down upon it all. The little one stretched out her hand towards them, and the match went out.

The Christmas lights rose higher and higher, till they looked to her like the stars in the sky. Then she saw a star fall, leaving behind it a bright streak of fire. "Someone is dying," thought the little girl, for her old grandmother, the only one who had ever loved her, and who was now dead, had told her that when a star falls, a soul was going up to God.

She again rubbed a match on the wall, and the light shone round her; in the brightness stood her old grandmother, clear and shining, yet mild and loving in her appearance. "Grandmother," cried the little one, "O take me with you; I know you will go away when the match burns out; you will vanish like the warm stove, the roast goose, and the large, glorious Christmas tree." And she made haste to light the whole bundle of matches, for she wished to keep her grandmother there. And the matches glowed with a light that was brighter than the noonday, and her grandmother had never appeared so large or so beautiful. She took the little girl in her arms, and they both flew upwards in brightness and joy far above the earth, where there was neither cold nor hunger nor pain, for they were with God.

In the dawn of morning there lay the poor little one, with pale cheeks and smiling mouth, leaning against the wall; she had been frozen to death on the last evening of the year; and the New year's sun rose and shone upon a little corpse! The child still sat, in the stiffness of death, holding the matches in her hand, one bundle of which was burnt. "She tried to warm herself," said some. No one imagined what beautiful things she had seen, nor into what glory she had entered with her grandmother, on New year's day.

THE ELVES AND THE SHOEMAKER

BY THE BROTHERS GRIMM

Once upon a time in a village far away, there was a poor shoemaker and his wife. The shoemaker worked very hard but there was never enough money. At last, one night, they had no food for their supper.

"All I have is enough leather to make one pair of shoes," he told his wife. He cut out the leather and placed it on the table.

"I will make them in the morning," he said. And they went to bed hungry.

In the morning, to his surprise, the leather had been made into a beautiful pair of shoes.

Jus then, a customer came in. "I have never seen such beautiful shoes!" she said. She gave the shoemaker three gold coins for them. With the money, the shoemaker's wife bought food and made a delicious dinner. The shoemaker bought more leather. That night, he cut the leather for two pairs of shoes.

In the morning, there were two pairs of shoes on the table! Soon two customers came in and bought the shoes. They each paid him well. So the shoemaker bought leather enough for three pairs more.

He cut out the work again that night, and found it finished in the morning. And so it went on for some time. Whatever he got ready at night was always done by morning, and the good man soon was rich.

One evening, at Christmas-time, he said to his wife, "Tonight let's sit up and watch, to see who it is that comes and does my work for me."

So they hid themselves behind a curtain to see what would happen.

As soon as the clock struck midnight, in came two little elves.

They sat on the shoemaker's bench and went to work. They stitched and rapped and hammered and tapped at such a rate that the shoemaker was amazed, and could not take his eyes off them for a moment.

On they went until the job was done, and the shoes stood ready on the table. Then they ran away as quick as lightning.

The next day the shoemaker said, "The elves have helped us. How can we help them?"

"I have an idea," said his wife. "It is so cold outside, and they have no coats to wear. I will make each of them a coat and a hat. And you can make each of them a little pair of shoes."

And so they did. That night they put two little hats and two little coats and two little pairs of shoes on the table. Then they went and hid behind the curtain to watch what the elves would do.

As the clock struck midnight, the elves came in and were going to sit down at their work as usual. But when they saw the clothes lying there for them, they laughed! They dressed themselves in the twinkling of an eye, and danced and skipped and sprang about as merry as could be.

At last they danced out the door. The shoemaker and his wife never saw them again. But everything went well with them as long as they lived.

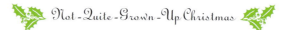

JINGLE BELL SLEIGH

Paint Palettes:

Deco Art:

Black Green
Black Plum
Bright Green
Cranberry Wine
Evergreen
Grey Sky
Mistletoe
Moon Yellow
Santa Red
Titanium White

Delta:

Adriatic Blue
Midnight Blue
JoSonja:
Pale Gold
Rich Gold

Supplies:

Wooden Sleigh

Note: All shading and highlighting floats should be kept "washy" and "layered" for greater color intensity.

Top and Bottom of Sleigh, including Runners:

1. Base-coat top and bottom of sleigh and both runners with Adriatic Blue.

2. Base edge of sleigh top and spindle between runners with Midnight Blue.

3. Add lettering around edge of sleigh top with Rich Gold. Add snowflakes with Titanium White.

4. Transfer Bell and Ribbon Pattern from page 175 onto top of sleigh. Transfer Pine Tree Landscape Pattern from pages 174–175 onto runners.

Ribbons:

1. Base-coat ribbons with Cranberry Wine. Dry-brush highlight with Santa Red, then again with Santa Red + Moon Yellow, then again with Santa Red + Moon Yellow (1:2).

2. Glaze over entire ribbon with Santa Red + Glazing Medium. Shade with Black Plum.

3. Using the hit/skip method, line with Black Plum.

Pine Sprigs:

1. Base-coat area where sprigs will be with Retarder. Base with Evergreen. Use a mop to soften and blend.

2. Line main stems for pine sprigs around bow with Black Green.

3. Pulling needles from each stem line outward, add a layer of needles to each stem with Evergreen. Add a second layer of needles with Mistletoe.

4. To separate some of the sprigs, float irregular lines across them with Black Green, thus creating two separate branches.

5. Pulling in opposite directions—from tip of needle back toward main stem—add a layer of needles with Bright Green. Make certain to cover hard Black Green floats with tips of strokes. This layer should not go all the way back to stem or center of sprig.

6. Add a few more needles on tips with Bright Green + Moon Yellow.

7. Shade behind ribbon and bells with Black.

Green Bells:

1. Base-coat bottom bell with Black Plum and remaining bells with Cranberry Wine.

2. Base-coat over all three bells with Rich Gold. Line centers with Pale Gold.

3. Shade bottom bell with Black Plum. Shade remaining bells with Cranberry Wine. Highlight with Pale Gold. Add reflected light on each bell with Titanium White + Adriatic Blue.

Cranberry Wine. Alternately line plaid pattern with Santa Red, Adriatic Blue, Mistletoe, and Rich Gold. Base hearts with Santa Red. Highlight with Santa Red + Moon Yellow. To make leaves, add double-loaded reverse teardrops loaded with Bright Green and tipped with Evergreen.

3. Alternately base-coat spindles with Santa Red, Bright Green, and Adriatic Blue.

Pine Tree Landscape:

1. Float hills with Grey Sky. Dry-brush tops of hills and tops and bottoms of runners with Titanium White. Darken behind some hills with Midnight Blue.

2. Line trunks and main branches on trees with Black Green, then again with Evergreen. Highlight center trees by lining tips of branches with Mistletoe, then again with Grey Sky. Highlight foreground trees by lining tips of branches with Bright Green, then again with Titanium White.

3. Splatter runners and top of sleigh with Titanium White.

4. Add holes on bells with Black Plum. Highlight left sides of holes with Cranberry Wine.

5. Add sprigs over ribbons and bells as in Pine Sprigs, Steps 1–6 on pages 172–173.

Seat Back:

1. Base-coat bottom piece of seat back with Evergreen. Using a #2 flat paintbrush, base checkerboard onto top with Adriatic Blue. Float holly leaves with Bright Green. Line leaves and veins with Bright Green. Dot berries with Santa Red. Shade with Black Plum.

2. Base-coat top piece of seat back with Santa Red, then again with two coats of

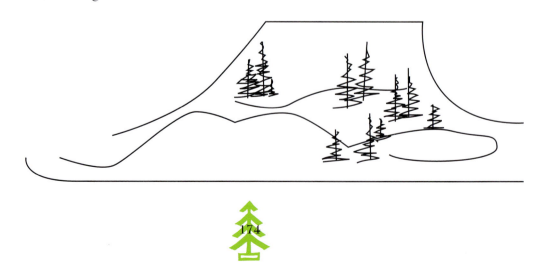

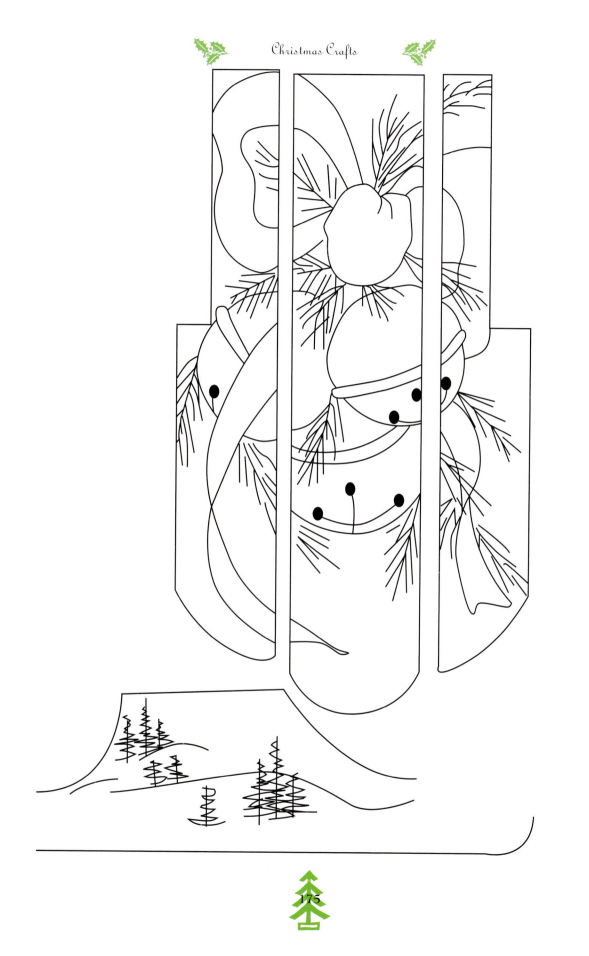

SANTA HAND PUPPET

One of the easiest ways to create a pro-fessional-looking hand puppet is to use a small gourd for the head. Ginger Summit, an accomplished gourd artist, has incor-porated the protruding stem end of the gourd to give this Santa a nose worthy of Jimmy Durante.

Materials & Tools

Small hard-shell gourd, cured and cleaned

Acrylic or tempera paints

Small paintbrush

Newspaper

Sewing thread

Sewing machine

Scrap of black fabric

⅓ yd. (30.5 cm) red fabric

¼ yd. (22.9 cm) polyester fleece

Electric drill with ¼" (6 mm) and ¹⁄₁₆"
(1.6 mm) bits

White glue

Metal skewer

Unspun wool fleece

Sharp knife

Keyhole saw

Curved tapestry needle

Heavy-gauge thread

1. Apply a base coat of acrylic paint to the gourd and allow it to dry.

2. After mixing the desired skin tone, paint the face area of the gourd. Use a mixture of pinks to give Santa his rosy glow. Allow the paint to dry; then add the eyes.

3. Using your own hand and arm to determine the measurements, draw a simple pattern for the robe on the newspaper (see figure 1). As a general guideline, the length of the fabric from the neck to the hem should be about 12" (30.5 cm), and you should allow about 3" (7.6 cm) for the neck to be attached to the puppet head. The distance between the puppet hands should be about 8" (20.3 cm). Before cutting the fabric, make sure the dimensions of your pattern fit both your hand and the puppet head. Don't forget to add a seam allowance of at least ¼" (6 mm) and a hem of about 1" (2.5 cm).

4. Cut two pieces of fabric for the robe and sew the shoulder and side seams. Then hem the bottom. Cut two narrow bands of polyester fleece and stitch them to the sleeves to make cuffs.

5. The hat is a semicircle of red fabric. Again make a newspaper pattern, drawing the semicircle to fit your gourd. Then cut the fabric and sew it into a cone. Add a band of polyester fleece around the bottom.

6. Cut two pieces for each mitten from the black fabric. After sewing the pieces together, turn the mittens right side out and attach them to the sleeves of the robe.

7. Using the ¼" (6 mm) bit, drill holes in all of the areas of the gourd where the hair and beard will be attached.

8. Put a dab of glue in one of the holes and use a skewer to push one end of a small amount of unspun wool fleece into the hole. Continue to fill all the holes with bits of wool. When all the hair is in place, let the glue dry completely.

9. Use the keyhole saw to cut a hole at the bottom of Santa's head, making the hole large enough to insert at least two fingers. Clean out all the seeds and pulp. Then drill ¹⁄₁₆" (1.6 mm) holes around the large hole, spacing them about 1" (2.5 cm) apart.

10. Using heavy-duty thread and a curved tapestry needle, stitch the robe onto the gourd through the small holes. Further anchor the fabric to the gourd with glue if desired.

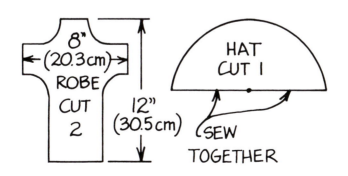

FIGURE 1

SOMERSAULTING SANTA

Simple toys are fun to make, and a tumbling Santa is certain to bring plenty of laughter to your holiday celebrations. To demonstrate how you might customize the decoration of your own Santa, designer Terry Taylor created two versions of this squeeze toy.

Materials & Tools

2 pieces ½" x 1³⁄₁₆" x 16" (1.3 x 2.1 x 40.6 cm) pine or basswood

1 sheet ⅛" x 4" x 24" (0.3 x 10.2 x 61 cm) basswood

½" x 1¾" x 1⅜" (1.3 x 4.4 x 3.5 cm) block of pine or basswood

⅛" dia. x ½" (0.3 x 1.5 cm) dowel

Acrylic paints

¼" (6 mm) soft brush

1" (2.5 cm) foam brush

Clear acrylic spray sealer

Gold stamp pad

Pencil with unused eraser

Electric drill with ¹⁄₁₆" (2 mm) and ⅛" (3 mm) bits

Motorized "mini-tool" or jigsaw

⅛" x 3" (0.3 x 7.6 cm) bolt, washer, nut, and finish washer

Pocketknife or carving knife

24" (61 cm) small-gauge copper or steel wire

Needle-nose pliers

Wire cutters

Small C-clamp

24" (61 cm) heavy carpet thread

1. Trace the pattern for the Santa figure onto the sheet of basswood and cut one body, two arms, and two legs using a motorized "mini-tool" or jigsaw. Sand all edges and surfaces and set aside.

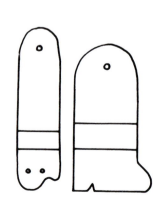

2. Mark the positions of the holes on the arms, body, and legs. Then, using a 1⁄16" (2 mm) bit, drill holes through the pieces.

3. Sand all surfaces of the two 16" (40.6 cm) pieces of wood. These are Santa's supports. Measure 1⁄2" (1.3 cm) down from one end of each support and center two marks spaced about 1⁄4" (6 mm) apart on the 11⁄16" (1.7 cm) face. Using the 1⁄16" bit, drill two holes on each piece as marked.

4. Measure 91⁄4" (23.5 cm) down from the end where you just drilled the two holes and center a mark. Use the 1⁄8" (3 mm) bit to drill a hole at the mark. Repeat this on the second support.

5. An optional decoration is to chip-carve the edges of the supports. Use a knife to make small V-cuts all along the edges.

6. Mark the center on the 1⅜" (3.5 cm) side of the small block. Using the ⅛" bit, drill a hole through the block at the mark.

7. Apply a base coat of acrylic paint to all the pieces and allow them to dry.

8. Using a pencil, lightly draw the outlines for the face, beard, boot, gloves, and belt onto the figure pieces. Then paint the features on all sides of the pieces as indicated, allowing them to dry between coats.

9. When the paint is dry, spray a light coat of the acrylic sealer on one side of each piece. Allow the sealer to dry before spraying the other side.

10. If you've chip-carved the edges of the supports, use a small brush and paint each V-cut. Allow it to dry.

11. Use the foam brush to paint the supports and the center block. By lightly applying the foam brush to each surface you will leave the small V-cuts untouched, revealing the contrasting color. Allow the paint to dry and apply a second coat if needed.

12. Draw a small star shape on the unused eraser. Using a craft knife, trim away the excess eraser around the star to make a rubber stamp.

13. Experiment with the cut eraser and a gold metallic stamp pad to determine how much to ink your rubber stamp. When sat-isfied with the results, decorate the sup-ports as desired.

Allow the ink to dry thoroughly before spraying it with acrylic sealer.

14. Cut four 2" (5.1 cm) lengths of wire. Using needle-nose pliers, twist two lengths together in the center for about ⅜" (1 cm). Repeat with the remaining two lengths.

15. Use the twisted wires to attach the arms and legs to the body. Thread one pair of wires through the top body hole, then through one arm on each side. Spread the ends of the wire apart to hold the arms in place. Repeat with the legs at the bottom hole. Trim the ends of the wire to about ¼" (6 mm). Your figure should move smoothly.

16. Paint the small dowel to match Santa's gloves. After the paint has dried, carefully apply glue to the ends of the dowel and place it between and slightly below the drilled holes of the gloves. Carefully clamp the assembly and allow the glue to dry.

17. Thread the bolt through the finish nut, the bottom hole in one support, the center block, and the second support. Finish with the small washer and nut.

18. Cut the carpet thread in half and thread each length through the small holes in the supports and through Santa's gloves. Tie off the ends securely.

19. Grasp the ends of the supports and give a gentle squeeze. As you continue to squeeze, Santa will begin to somersault!

HOT GLUE AND GLITTER WREATH

So you want to make just one more wreath. But you have nothing to use for a base. You're out of greenery and flowers. All the ornaments are hung on the tree. And the last of the ribbon was used long ago. There's nothing left but some paint, glitter, and a glue gun. Believe it or not, you have the makings for a wreath!

This probably isn't a wreath you'd want to hang on your front door, but it illustrates a handy technique for making letters, numbers, and all sorts of other shapes to decorate your holiday creations. Simply coat a piece of glass with cooking oil spray and squirt hot glue around and around to form a circle, dropping glitter between each layer. Once it cools, the glue lifts off easily and can be painted on the back to add color. This "wreath" took a little over three 10" (25 cm) sticks of hot glue.

SANTA'S PALACE

Add some turrets and flags to the top of your roof, cover everything in a frosty coat of white, and there's no doubt about it—you've combined the essential ingredients for a palace way up north.

Complete the magical scene with a gingerbread cookie Santa and his sleigh out front, attaching the lead deer to a nearby tree to make them look as if they're ready to "dash away all."

CANDY LAND CHRISTMAS

One way to come up with a concept for your gingerbread creation is to let the candy be your guide. For a charmingly tidy look, stick with a color scheme (like the bright palette of pastels featured here). You can also allow the shape and style of the candy itself to determine design detail. The fruit candy on this house cries out to form scalloped edges on the roof, and the bright candy bits in the window boxes shape themselves into the most imaginative of flowers.

Lollipops, like the cone-shaped pastel swirls in this display, come in all shapes and sizes, and many of them are a wonderful material for trees. However, if you're entering a contest that tells you all parts of your gingerbread creation must be edible (or if you simply want to pass the edible test yourself), you'll need to remove the suckers' sticks. Pop them in a microwave for just a few seconds to soften them up, then carefully twist them until the sticks pull out.

Want to add a dash of realism to your candy-land fantasy? Try licorice root for an authentic-looking woodpile.

MERRY·GO·ROUND

Merry is definitely the word. This festive carousel is a snap to bake and assemble. Use all your leftover good cheer to create bright-colored frosting for carousel paint, then decorate your horses for a Christmas carnival. Cookie cutters come in myriad animal shapes, too, if you want to add a few more figures to the celebration.

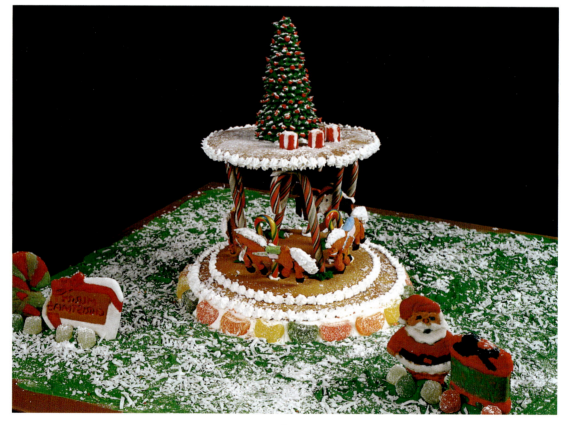

Appendix of Techniques

The Appendix is filled with tips and techniques that will help you create many of the projects pictured in this book. The first section teaches you how to make a basic gingerbread house and the nuts and bolts of decorating gingerbread houses. From there, you can model your house after one of the ones featured or you can use your imagination to create your own masterpiece. The second section offers the essentials to craft wreaths, garlands, and swags along with tips to wrap packages and create some of the ornaments featured. The third section provides general instructions on tole-painting, beginning with what materials you need and then offering tips to improve your technique.

GINGERBREAD BAKING & BUILDING
BASIC TECHNIQUES AND TEMPLATES

In this section, we take you through all the steps of creating the basic house you see pictured on the facing page. Templates you can reproduce for the entire structure, including the chimney and porch, appear on pages 186–188.

Chances are, you'll enjoy the exper-ience of baking and building a gingerbread house most if you can spread it out over several days. Here's a rough schedule.

• Allow 30 minutes for mixing your dough, plus at least three hours more to refrigerate it.

• Plan two hours for rolling, cutting, and baking the dough, and another four hours for letting it cool.

• Budget about an hour and a half for assembling your house, including time for it to dry and settle between stages.

Creating Your Pattern Pieces
What You Will Need

Pencil
Pen
Ruler or straightedge
Graph paper (optional)
Cardboard or other sturdy material (such as poster board or file folders)
Tape

We've provided a pattern for a basic house, along with a porch and a chimney. Together, they create a structure that is 9 x 9 inches (22.5 x 22.5 cm) at the base and stands about 10 inches (25 cm) tall from the bottom of the porch to the tip of the chimney. The design is both manageable for beginners and full of features that allow for lots of original decorating touches. It's also easy to adapt if you've got something different in mind but want a starting point.

Simply trace the templates onto cardboard or any other stiff material, and cut them out. If you're adapting the templates or creating something differ-ent, you may want to measure your pieces on graph paper first, then create them on a stiffer paper. Then—and this step is important—construct your house out of cardboard and masking tape before you even think about dough and icing.

BASIC HOUSE PATTERN

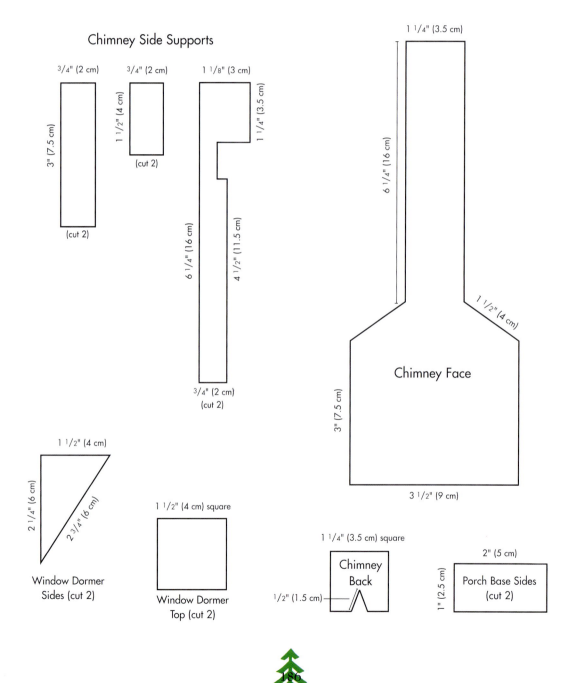

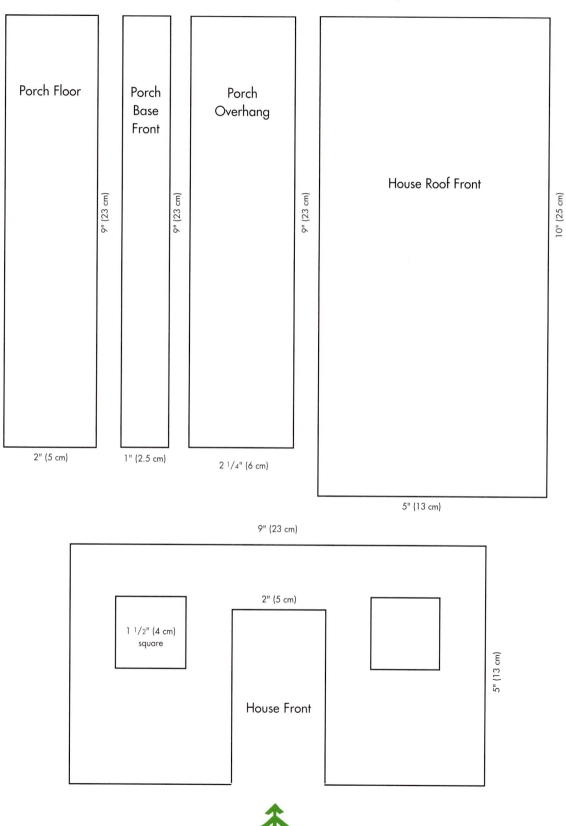

Porch Floor

9" (23 cm)

2" (5 cm)

Porch Base Front

9" (23 cm)

1" (2.5 cm)

Porch Overhang

9" (23 cm)

2 1/4" (6 cm)

House Roof Front

10" (25 cm)

5" (13 cm)

9" (23 cm)

2" (5 cm)

1 1/2" (4 cm) square

House Front

5" (13 cm)

187

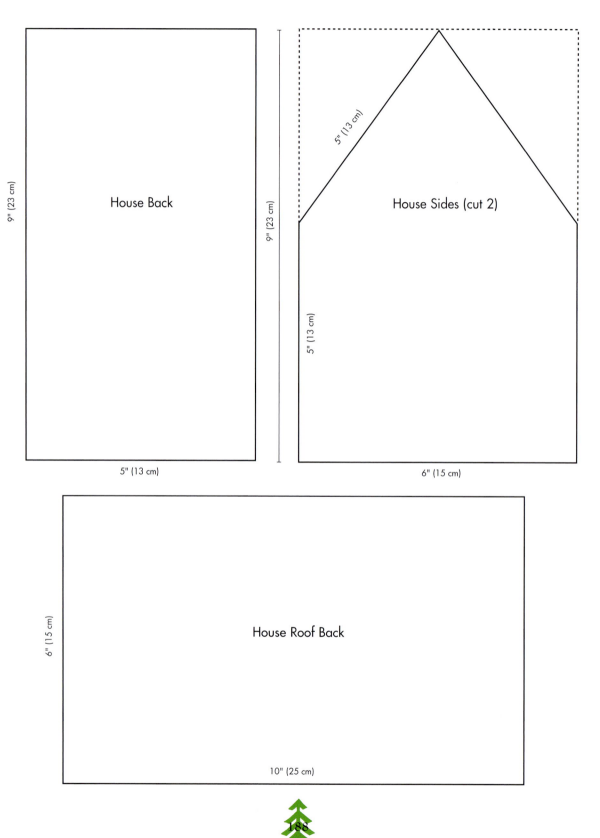

House Back

9" (23 cm)

5" (13 cm)

House Sides (cut 2)

9" (23 cm)

5" (13 cm)

5" (13 cm)

6" (15 cm)

House Roof Back

6" (15 cm)

10" (25 cm)

Rolling out the Dough

What you will need

Flat surface
Rolling pin
Flour
Baking-grade parchment paper (you can use aluminum foil as a substitute)
Gingerbread dough

A baking board is ideal, but any clean flat surface will do for rolling out your dough. Cover your surface with parchment paper, place a portion of dough on top of it, and begin rolling out the dough with a floured rolling pin. Roll out a portion large enough for a couple of pattern pieces at a time.

Two things to keep in mind:

1. You want the dough piece you're rolling out to be as square and even as possible—and slightly larger than the pattern pieces you plan to cut from it.

2. Your rolled-out dough should be approximately $1/2$ inch (1.3 cm) thick if your goal is stability. For accent pieces (not the main supporting walls of your house), you can roll the dough a bit thinner if you want a more delicate look.

Cutting Out Your House

What You Will Need

Flour
Gingerbread house pattern pieces
Pizza wheel
Small paring knife
Pastry brush
Airtight container for excess dough

Lightly dust the surface of your dough with flour to prevent the pattern pieces from sticking. Then, place as many pattern pieces as will fit on your rolled-out dough and, using the patterns as a guide, begin cutting your dough pieces. A floured pizza wheel works best on larger pieces, since knives can drag and misshape the dough. A small paring knife is perfect for smaller pieces and more intricate cuts, such as those on the chimney. Peel away your excess dough and save it in an airtight container. It will come in handy for creating decorations or, better yet, for a batch of cookies when you need fortitude later.

Use plenty of flour as you roll out the dough.

Roll gingerbread slightly larger than the pattern pieces.

Roll dough to $1/2$-inch (1.3 cm) thick for main support walls.

A small paring knife works well on smaller pieces and intricate cuts.

A floured pizza wheel works best on larger pieces.

Decorating Details: You can score or texturize pieces of unbaked dough so they resemble bricks, wooden planks, or other building materials. To make colored pieces, you can also brush liquid food coloring, watered-down gel coloring, or food coloring paste mixed with water on the dough before baking it. For example, by scoring your chimney piece and coloring it red, you can create a brick chimney effect.

For the basic house pattern, you'll need two 4-inch-tall (10 cm) supports for your porch. Peppermint sticks and other candies are options, or you may want to create gingerbread columns. If so, hand roll two ½-inch-thick (1.3 cm) pieces in the shape of bread sticks.

Transferring and Baking Your House Pieces

What You Will Need

Scissors
Flat cookie sheets

Cut the parchment paper around your individual house pieces, and transfer them—paper and all—to flat cookie sheets. Space your pieces so they're about an inch (2.5 cm) apart, trying to keep larger pieces and smaller pieces on separate trays, since they may finish baking at different times.

Tips:

Use a pastry brush to dust any excess flour off the dough before baking it; otherwise the flour will cake on.

If you've got time, after you've cut out your dough pieces, let them sit out, uncovered, for several days before you bake them. The settling process helps them retain their shape.

—Judy Searcy

Before beginning your house, bake a batch of gingerbread cookies to test your dough recipe and become familiar with working with gingerbread.

—Bill Bena

The colder your dough, the better it will retain its shape. Leave any dough you're not working with in the refrigerator until you're ready to roll it out.

Use plenty of flour as you roll out the dough. The more you work with it, the softer—and stickier—the dough gets.

Bake the gingerbread in an oven preheated to 350°F (177°C) until the dough is deep brown but not black (approximately 20 minutes). If you decide your pieces aren't quite done after they've cooled, stick them back in the oven for a few minutes.

Remove the cookie sheets from the oven, and allow the pieces to cool approximately 25 minutes before transferring them to a flat countertop or board. (If the surface is uneven, it could cause the pieces to crack or break.) Allow the pieces to cool for four hours minimum (overnight if possible) before beginning to assemble your house.

Tips:

Soft gingerbread will sabotage your housebuilding efforts. Bake your dough until it's completely dry and crisp.

Use completely flat cookie sheets. If they're bowed, they could cause your pieces to break.

We recommend cutting your house pieces before you bake them (rather than baking a flat sheet of dough and cutting the pieces out of the warm, baked gingerbread). But you can do some quick nips and tucks to the just-from-the-oven gingerbread. Place your templates back on top of the warm pieces to see if the dough expanded while baking, and trim them back into shape if necessary. You could also save some of the intricate cuts, such as windows and doors, for this stage.

Always leave your gingerbread in the oven a little longer than the recipe says, even if it smells like it's burning, just to make sure it's extra hard.

—Kristen Cook

Decorating Detail: If you want your house to have a rougher, more textured look, use the sides of the pieces that baked against the cookie sheet as the outside of your house.

The Assembly

What You Will Need

Base

Pencil

Baked house pieces, plus two 4-inch (10 cm) porch supports

Royal icing

Pastry bag and #7 plain writing tip (plus a damp cloth to keep the pastry bag covered when you're not using it)

Serrated knife

Ruler for evening up some of your pieces, if necessary

Pastry brush for dusting crumbs as you work

Several temporary braces spice jars, cans, or boxes of raisins will do (optional).

Choosing a Base

Anything flat or sturdy will work as a base. The house we're assembling will easily fit on a large serving platter, which can be covered with frosting once your house is complete. Or, you might want

Tools for assembling your house.

to purchase a cake board (available at cake decorating shops) or cut out a wooden base and cover it with a decorative material such as gold foil. One-inch-thick (2.5 cm) polystyrene is another good choice for a base, especially if you plan to include lots of posted objects (such as candy cane trees) in your landscaping—you can stick them right in the base rather than securing them with icing. Finishing the edges of your base (by painting them to match the base surface or covering them with a decorative foil or paper, for example) lends polished appeal to your entire gingerbread display.

Before You Begin

Review The Trimmings (beginning on page 196) before you start assembling your house, giving some thought to how you plan to decorate. Some of the decorating techniques, such as attaching marzipan windows or piping lattice icing on the front of the porch, are easiest if you work with flat pieces of gingerbread before they are part of the assembled house.

Piping Primer

A 12-inch (30 cm) pastry bag is a good size for both building and decorating. Fit your pastry bag with a coupler and the decorating tip you want to use, fold the sides of the bag down about one third of the way, and use a spatula to fill the bag half full with icing. Be sure to push the icing down into the tip to avoid air pockets; then twist the end of the bag to seal it. To pipe, apply pressure to the end of the bag and continue twisting it as it empties.

If you've never used a pastry bag to pipe icing before, you'll easily get the hang of it. But don't attempt your first flourish on your house's main entrance; practice techniques and styles on a sheet of wax paper first.

Building

1. Begin by lightly marking in pencil where you want the house to sit on the base. Don't forget the porch along the front. Your pattern can help you establish positions.

2. Start with the back and one side piece of your house. Pipe icing along the bottom edges, then place them over the pencil marks you made for them, forming a corner. Hold them in place several seconds until the icing begins to harden. You can also prop them in place with your temporary braces, though chances are the icing will set up so quickly this won't be necessary. See photos 1 and 2.

3. Pipe icing along the end and bottom of the other side piece and press it in place, gently holding the joints until the piece is secure. Continue until your four front and back pieces and the base of your porch are in place. Since royal icing is the glue that holds your house together, be sure to pipe a liberal amount everywhere gingerbread meets gingerbread, then go back over some of the edges, especially on the inside base of your house, for reinforcement. See photos 3–8.

4. Let your house and porch dry 30 minutes minimum—overnight if possible—before adding the roof, porch overhang, and chimney.

5. Attach the porch overhang before placing the front of the roof on the house. First, position your porch supports (gingerbread columns or candy posts). If you have to shave some length off your

> ### Tip:
> To help stabilize your structure while your royal icing is drying, use straight pins or quilter's pins (which are long and have large heads) to temporarily hold your walls together.
>
> —Sally Fredrickson

Photo 1: *Start with back and side piece.*

Photo 2: *Hold and pipe pieces in place.*

Photo 3: *Add other side and front.*

Photo 4: *Attach porch sides.*

Photo 5: *Pipe additional icing.*

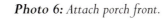

Photo 6: *Attach porch front.*

Photo 7: *Add porch floor.*

Photo 8: *Settle it into place.*

Photo 9: *Position porch supports.*

Photo 10: *Set porch overhang in place.*

Photo 11: *Shave front roof piece, if necessary, before attaching.*

Photo 12: *Pipe icing for back roof piece.*

Photo 13: *Add back roof piece.*

Photo 14: *Attach lower chimney side supports.*

Photo 15: *Attach chimney to face of house.*

Photo 16: *Add middle side supports.*

Photo 17: *Attach notched side supports.*

Photo 18: *Fit tiny notched piece over roof tip.*

Photo 19: *Cover the roof with icing.*

Photo 20: *Add window dormers.*

porch supports, use a serrated knife on the ginger-bread columns or a heated knife on the candy canes. (You may want to insert the supports temporarily to help the overhang settle into place; remove them when you decorate the front of your house, then put them back in permanently and secure them with icing.) Pipe icing along the top edge of the front house piece. Set the porch overhang in place, then attach the front of the roof, which should rest on top of the overhang. You may also need to shave your roof pieces slightly to ensure a snug fit. See photos 9–11.

6. Attach the back of the roof by piping icing along the slanted edges of the back side, then pressing the longer roof piece on the slants so that the peak is even with the front and back points. You should have a one-inch (2.5 cm) overhang in the back. See photos 12 and 13. If your roof piece needs some support to keep it from sliding as it settles, use a soda can or a box of brown sugar.

7. To fit the chimney on the side of the house, first attach the $^3/_4$-inch-wide x 3-inch-tall (1.9 cm x 7.5 cm) side supports to the chimney face piece. Next, pipe icing along the outer edges of these lower side supports and use them to attach the chimney face to the house. Attach the $^3/_4$-inch-wide x 1 $^1/_2$-inch-tall (1.9 cm x 3.8 cm) side supports and the 6 $^1/_4$-inch (15.7 cm) side supports. The notches in the longer pieces, which fit over the lip of the roof, will likely have to be shaved slightly so that they fit snugly in place. Finally, fit the tiny piece with an inverted "V" notch over the peak of the roof to form the fourth side of the chimney. See photos 14–18.

8. For each window dormer, attach two triangle pieces to the roof 1$^1/_2$ inches (3.8 cm) apart (the longest side attaches to the roof), and place a square piece on top of them. You can also cover the entire roof in a blanket of royal icing snow, as we did, and simply position the pieces of the window dormers in the icing. See photos 19 and 20.

The Trimmings

What You Will Need

Royal Icing (recipe on page 208)

Pastry bag and decorating tips (We recommend a #21 star tip, a #16 star tip, a #7 plain tip, a #2 plain tip, and a #352 leaf tip to get started.)

Damp cloth to keep pastry bag covered when you're not using it.

Small, angled spatula for spreading icing

Food coloring (food coloring comes in multiple colors and various forms, including liquid, paste, powder, and gel. Powder is best for coloring chocolates, while paste or gel is ideal for icings.)

Assortment of all things edible (candy, crackers, cookies, cereal… you get the idea. The more unusual the better, and the more in general, the merrier.)

Wax paper (optional)

Let your newly assembled house settle for at least an hour, or overnight if you can stand it. Once it's dry and stable, you're ready to start decking the halls—not to mention the walls, windows, doorways, and yard—anywhere icing will stick and some piece of food you're transforming into a shingle or stone will hold.

Roof Décor

The big open space of your roof calls out for imaginative adornment. If you want your roof to look realistic, consider crackers or shredded wheat squares for a thatched motif. Layered Necco wafers or wafer cookies are popular for creating a more colorful, shingled style. You may simply want to frost your entire roof in white royal icing and pipe a scalloped design with chocolate. Or, drip icicles from your window dormers and "let it snow."

Tips:

Always brace the insides of walls, especially tall ones—with bread sticks, thick pretzel sticks, extra pieces of gingerbread, or some other material. If your house is sturdy, you can relax and enjoy decorating.

—Elizabeth Ascik

If your house pieces are not fitting together evenly, use a serrated knife to straighten up your edges. Be sure to shave the pieces carefully, or more brittle pieces might break. For intricate adjustments, sandpaper or even an emery board will work well. A craft grinder is also a great tool for shaving off pieces of baked gingerbread and whittling down candy canes.

If you're transporting your house to another location, maybe to a competition or so that it can serve as a centerpiece at a party or a prize in an auction, assemble everything but the roof and fragile landscaping pieces at home; then attach the roof and finish your decorating on site, if possible.

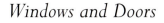
Windows and Doors

You can attach window shapes to the flat house pieces before your structure is assembled, or add them once it's standing. Roll a thin layer of marzipan, and cut out shapes to fill your windows. Secure them in place with royal icing, and pipe in chocolate frames or even colored curtains or candles that look like they're positioned on the inside sill.

Most any sort of wafer cookie or thin candy bar can be used as a propped-open front door or for window shutters. You can also bake your own doors and shutters out of gingerbread, and decorate them with icing and candy.

Adding a door made of licorice iced on a gingerbread base.

Attaching shutters.

The Edibility Issue

One of the most commonly asked questions about gingerbread houses is: Can you really eat them? The answer you're likely to get from anyone who has put the time and effort into making one is: Yes, but don't you dare dig into mine.

The tradition behind gingerbread houses is that they're made entirely out of items you can eat, from the gingerbread and icing structure to the candy trim. But since so much work goes into them (and because many of the ingredients lose their freshness during the assembly process), people seldom see gingerbread houses as something to snack on. Typically, they're left intact as holiday centerpieces.

Purists in Asheville, North Carolina are diligent about their display's edibility, down to the last candy wrapper and sucker stick (removing both). Others say it's okay to use a polystyrene base for a tree here, a piece of wood for support there, or nonfood trinkets and toys for decoration all over. And those from either camp who want their house to stand for seasons to come may choose to spray the finished product with an effective but less-than-tasty coating of shellac.

Melted Candy Windows

To make candy windows that look like stained glass, follow the procedure shown here. First, cut out your window shapes and begin baking your gingerbread. While it's baking, use a hammer to crush colored candies in their wrappers. Remove the gingerbread piece with window openings from the oven when approximately 10 minutes of baking time remain. Fill the openings with crushed candy, bringing the candy level with the surface of the gingerbread. Stick everything back in the oven for the last 10 minutes of baking, and the candy will melt into colored glass window panes. Keep a careful watch during the final stage of baking. If left in the oven too long, the melting candy may flow out of the window openings.

Poured sugar windows are a more advanced variation on the melted candy theme. Combine 1 $1/4$ cups (250 g) of granulated sugar, $1/2$ cup (170 g) of corn syrup and $1/3$ cup (80 mL) of water in a saucepan and heat the ingredients gently, stirring constantly, until the sugar dissolves. Bring the mixture to a boil, and cook it without stirring until the temperature reaches 310°F (154°C) (using a candy

Crush colored hard candy.

Remove stray bits of candy before baking.

Fill the window openings.

Bake approximately 10 minutes, then cool to harden before handling.

Window Repairs

Candy windows can crack and break, and they're especially prone to melting in humidity. If you have to whip up a quick replacement, measure the size of your frame, then use sticks of gum, licorice, or any sticky, pliable substance to create a shape identical to your window frame. Make a small batch of poured sugar or melt crushed hard candy in the microwave, then pour the melted mixture into the temporary gum or licorice frame. Once your replacement window is hard and cool, you can peel it off the makeshift frame and ice it into its permanent position on your house.

Making a Paper Piping Cone

For delicate details that require fine piping, either you can use a pastry bag and the tiniest tip you can find, or you can practice some easy kitchen origami and create your own cone. Start with parchment paper, then follow the steps shown here.

Step 1: Fold parchment paper to create a triangle.

Step 2: Flatten the edge with a knife.

Step 3: Cut the triangle out of the larger piece of paper.

Step 4: Bring one point from the base of the triangle up to the top point.

Step 5: Wrap the other base point around and up to the back of the top point.

Step 6: Shuffle the paper so that the inside piece is tightening while the outer piece continues to wrap. The action forms a tight tip.

Step 7: Fold the pieces at the top of the cone to hold the shape in place.

thermometer to measure the temperature). With great care (and oven mitts!), pour the boiling sugar into your window forms. Kids need adult help if they're going to try this technique.

Color Flow

For decorative surfaces with a smooth sheen (like the bright yellow windows shown here), use the color flow technique we've illustrated. Create a thin royal icing by combining a one-pound box (454 g) of confectioners' sugar, two tablespoons of meringue powder, and approximately three teaspoons of water. Beat the mixture on a low speed for about 20 minutes, adding more water as you mix if the color flow seems to be too thick. (Beating it on a low speed for a good length of time will help prevent the piped-on color flow from developing air bubbles.) When you've finished mixing, add food coloring, if you like.

With a pencil, draw the pattern you want to create on a piece of wax paper. Pipe your thin icing onto the border of your pattern first, using a #3 or #4 decorating tip or a handmade paper cone (the goal here is a thin, fine line), then fill in the interior. Let your first color dry thoroughly before adding accents in a new color. Be sure to let your entire creation dry completely (at least 48 hours), or it

Pipe a thin border around your design.

Fill the interior.

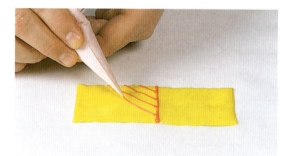

Let the first color dry thoroughly before adding another.

Let the entire piece dry at least 48 hours before handling.

Tip:

Visit candy stores for inspiration. Browse the aisles of the places that sell in bulk, and you're bound to leave with a new idea or two for shingling your roof (try sticks of red gum curled up at the ends), shuttering your windows (how about chocolate bars?), or even paving the path to your door (the darker colors of gourmet jelly beans make great gravel; so does sundae topping).

Making a wreath.

Let the wreath dry completely before handling it.

will crack immediately when you try to remove it from the wax paper. Even when they're dry, color flow pieces will be brittle, so handle them with care when you pick them up and ice them into place.

Wreaths and Garlands

With a #352 leaf tip, you can pipe colored royal icing garlands directly onto your porch—or on a fence or gate in the yard. You can also create wreaths by piping circles onto wax or parchment paper. Apply candy decorations before the icing hardens, then let the wreaths dry completely (overnight if you've got the time) before moving them from the paper to their hanging positions on the house.

Attach the wreath with royal icing.

Different tips create different piping designs for borders and trim.

Piping lattice.

Piping trim.

Piping icicles.

Icing Trim

Regardless of how you choose to decorate, piping swirls of icing along all the edges, seams, and borders of your house (from doors and windows to the edges of the roof) both provides a finished look and helps reinforce the structure. The icing tips we recommend—attached to a pastry bag—will get you started on a basic variety of decorative borders.

Icing can also be used to pipe everything from a lattice pattern on the base of your front porch or on your window shutters (it's best to do this before attaching those pieces) to icicles hanging from the roof. For the icicles, pipe a base dot, then drip the icing down from there. A #2 plain tip is good for making smaller icicles.

Building Materials

Give yourself a little time, and you'll start to view the grocery store as a fully stocked home and building supply center. Pretzels, for example, are ideal fence-building material. Post them in mini-marshmallows, then fuse rails together with royal icing for a split-rail look. Tootsie Rolls can be softened in the microwave for a few seconds, then shaped into everything from stumps to wood piles.

You can also craft custom-designed bricks, stones, logs, and texturized surfaces out of gingerbread dough, then ice them on where you want them. Brush the building-materials-to-be with food coloring, if you like, before baking them. For a sturdy log cabin, attach rolled-dough logs to your house pieces, then bake them into place. Create a brick surface without the time-consuming task of mortaring individual pieces by scoring the dough with a knife (or using a purchased mold to make brick-like impressions) before it goes in the oven.

To create stones that will pass for real rocks, knead natural-colored marzipan with marzipan you've colored in darker shades, marbling the two together. Chocolate-covered raisins and walnut pieces work well, too.

will survive the baking process.) Then, grease the foil or paper lightly before adding the dough. You can rest the entire contraption on chopsticks so one side of your rounded structure won't flatten as it bakes.

Marzipan "stones" cover the chimney.

Cutting strips.

Chocolate-covered raisins provide facing for the foundation.

Draping strips over a foil-covered can and pipe.

Pretzels set into mini-marshmallows make a good fence.

Creating Rounded Structures

For turrets and other rounded gingerbread structures, simply drape pieces of dough over cans (soda and coffee cans are perfect) and around pipes, then bake them into shape. Cover the base first with aluminum foil or parchment paper. (Masking tape is fine to hold the foil or paper in place. And yes, it

A variety of cylindrical and cone-shaped gingerbread pieces.

Landscaping

Upside-down sugar cones are the perfect shape for evergreen trees. Cover them with points of green-colored royal icing (using a #352 leaf tip), and decorate them with candy ornaments such as Red Hots. If you're willing to add inedible pieces to your display, craft stores sell different sizes of polystyrene cones—good to use if you decide to create an entire forest. Or, simplify the process considerably and stand up suckers and lollipops as instant trees. Marshmallows coated with royal icing and covered with green-colored coconut give you shrubs with plenty of texture to line a path or border a fence.

Create a skating pond by spreading waves of blue-colored royal icing on your base or by coloring corn syrup and pouring it into a bordered area. Consider lining your pond with gumdrop rocks or crumbled gingerbread gravel, and toss some sugar crystals on top for chunks of frosty ice.

For a lamppost, stick a chocolate-covered confectioners' stick in a base of royal icing, then use another drop of icing to mount a candy ball (small jawbreakers work well) on top of the stick.

A sugar cone as an evergreen base.

A skating pond made of blue royal icing.

Tip:

Sprinkle everything with confectioners' sugar when you're finished, and your entire gingerbread scene will look like it's just been dusted with snow.

The most important thing is not to rush when you're assembling and decorating your house. I always leave a few days at the end for last-minute touch-ups. Thinking up new and creative decorations is what keeps it fun.

—David Handermann

Marzipan Figures

A bit like edible play dough, marzipan is a pliable candy that can be rolled, pressed, and molded into the shapes of people, packages, and creatures great and small. It's easiest if you have several colored batches (such as brown and red in addition to natural) within reach when you're working on your figures. A recipe appears on page 215. Photos here show the steps to making a marzipan dog.

First knead the marzipan to soften it.

Roll out marzipan pieces for the dog's body, head, ears, tongue, tail, and collar.

Slit open both ends of the body to create front and back legs, and to create a mouth on the head.

Add the tail and collar.

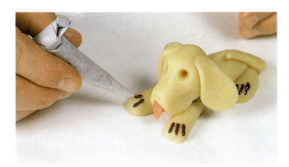

Add the tongue and ears to the head, create eyeholes, and pipe chocolate to accent the eyes, nose, and paws.

Pastillage is perfect for making curved forms and simulating draped fabric.

Pastillage drying as it is molded over a cylinder. It will harden in minutes.

Pastillage Figures

Pastillage, similar to stiff putty, is sometimes referred to as gum paste. You can shape it into curving architectural structures, drape it in the form of blankets, or swirl it around a snowman's neck as a scarf. Whatever you make will harden in minutes into a durable, snow-white decoration, which you can frost, paint with food coloring, or leave as is. Best of all, pastillage is a cinch to make; follow the recipe on page 209.

Fondant Figures

A close cousin of pastillage, fondant is also in demand for its bright white color and malleability. Unlike pastillage, however, it contains fat. While it will hold its shape (somewhat like soft clay), it will never harden into as rigid a form as pastillage will. Premade fondant is available at cake decorating shops (in white and various colors, flavored and unflavored). You can also make your own, using the recipe on page 209.

Melted Chocolate Features

There's not much in life that can't be made better with a dose of chocolate. And so it goes with gingerbread décor. Melted chocolate, which you can pour, pipe, or dip into, provides just the touch of silky luxury you may be looking for. You can get standard cooking chocolate in wafers and chunks, and in white (which can be colored to match almost any shade) and dark. It's just the thing for dipping and simple piping.

Kristen Cook used melted baking chocolate on her Avonlea Inn (page 68) to coat the porch pillars. She simply dipped bread sticks down in it. ("It provided a much smoother finish than icing.") She also put it in a pastry bag and, with a tiny tip, piped the inn's widow's walk and porch railing. To do something similar, draw the pattern you want to follow, whether it's crisscrosses or elaborate curlicues, on

Fondant is malleable like pastillage, but does not harden into a rigid form.

Because it contains fat, fondant is glossy.

A snowman made of fondant (left), and figures shaped of pastillage.

a sheet of white paper. Cover it with see-through wax paper, then pipe according to your design. Freeze the piped chocolate for about an hour, then carefully peel your delicate pieces off the wax paper and put them in place.

If you want to create super-sturdy, stand-alone structures, you'll have the best results if you use the highest-grade chocolate ("couverture," it's called), and "temper" it properly. (Tempering is a heating and cooling process that requires a candy thermometer as a gauge and the simple instructions in a candymaking book as a guide.)

Lighting a House

Just as real-life houses that look warm and welcoming when lights are burning inside, a gingerbread house with see-through windows and an inside light has added charm. Here's how to outfit your house with a burning bulb.

1. Think ahead. The time to decide you want to light your house from within is before you've put it together. You'll want to choose a base in which you can cut a hole and prepare it for a light set before you put up your walls.

2. Purchase an inexpensive light set at a craft shop; it will include a bulb, its base, and a cord.

3. Cut a hole in your house base to accommodate the light set. So that the light cord won't prevent your base from sitting flat, you'll also want to either carve a groove along the underside of the base (easy to do if your base is polystyrene), or equip your base with feet so the cord can wind under it.

4. Once your house is assembled, insert the bulb and its base through the hole you've prepared, and plug it in.

Gingerbread Dough

This recipe makes enough dough for the basic house, porch, and chimney shown on pages 187–189. A heavy-duty mixer will ease the dough-making process.

Cream until light and fluffy:

2 sticks (1 cup or 230 g) butter
3/4 cup (100 g) firmly packed brown sugar

Add and blend on low speed:

3/4 cup (250 g) molasses

Sift, add, and blend until all the flour is absorbed:

5 1/4 cups (630 g) all-purpose flour
2 teaspoons baking soda
2 teaspoons cinnamon
2 teaspoons ground ginger
1/2 teaspoon ground cloves
1 teaspoon salt

Add and blend:

3/4 cup (177 ml) cold water

Spread the dough out on a sheet pan, cover it tightly with plastic wrap, and refrigerate it until you're ready to roll it out (ideally overnight; three hours minimum). It should keep well in the refrigerator for approximately three days.

Tip:

Softening your butter by getting it to room temperature before beginning the creaming process will give you a helpful head start—especially if you're kneading by hand.

Royal Icing

You should have enough icing to construct and decorate your basic house, porch, and chimney with this recipe. However, because the icing will eventually dry out, you might make just half the recipe for constructing your house, then whip up the second half when you're ready to decorate.

5 1/4 cups (630 g) confectioners' sugar
1 tablespoon and 1 1/2 teaspoons cream of tartar
1/2 cup egg whites (120 mL)

Sift the sugar after measuring it. Add the egg whites and cream of tartar to the sugar mixture. Combine the ingredients with a hand mixer on low speed, then beat them on high for two to five minutes, until they're snow-white and fluffy.

Keep your icing bowl covered with a damp towel to retain moisture; the mixture forms a crust quickly when it's exposed to air.

Marzipan

8 ounces (237 g) almond paste (You can purchase premade paste in most gourmet groceries or cake decorating shops.)
2 tablespoons corn syrup
1 1/2 cups (180 g) confectioners' sugar (sifted)

Mix the almond paste and corn syrup on low speed until they form a smooth and very tight mixture. You may have to knead the ingredients by hand to blend the mixture completely. Add sugar, a bit at a time, as fast as it's absorbed. Stop when the mixture is stiff but still workable and not too dry. If it crusts over before you use it, microwave it for a couple of seconds before you begin working with it.

Pastillage

1 tablespoon gelatin
1/4 cup plus 2 tablespoons (89 mL) water
4 1/2 cups (540 g) confectioners' sugar

Dissolve the gelatin in the water, then add the confectioners' sugar. Keep the mixture covered with a wet towel to prevent it from drying out. The surface may still crust a bit, so sprinkle some more confectioners' sugar in, and knead the pastillage just before using it.

Fondant

8 tablespoons (1 stick) unsalted butter
3/4 teaspoon vanilla
1/4 teaspoon salt
2/3 cup (225 g) sweetened condensed milk
5 cups (600 g) sifted confectioners' sugar

Beat the first three ingredients until they're soft, then add the sweetened condensed milk slowly and beat the mixture until it's very light. Add the confectioners' sugar, cup by cup. Dust your work surface with another cup (120 g) of confectioners' sugar, turn your fondant out onto the surface, and work the sugar into it with your hands. As with pastillage, the surface of your fondant may crust as it sits. If so, sprinkle it with additional confectioners' sugar and knead it just before using it.

Tips for Arrangements, Topiaries, Garlands, Swags, Ornaments, Gift Wrap, Flowers and Bows

Basics:

Glue Guns

A glue gun may not be the most fun you can have for under $10, but it's close. Fast, easy to use, and incredibly flexible, it will affix almost anything to almost anything else.

In this book, designers used glue guns to attach flowers, herbs, cones, nuts, seeds, pods, bows, ribbons, lace, twigs, vines, lichens, and birds (fake, of course) to bases of foam, moss, vine, straw, and plastic.

To use a glue gun, simply insert a glue stick, plug in the gun, and wait for it to heat. Then aim and squeeze the trigger. Hold the glued items together for half a minute or so, until the bond is firm.

Tips

• Cover the work area with newspaper. Almost all glue guns drip.

• A glue gun that can stand up when you set it down is extremely convenient. When shopping for a gun, check to see whether it has a stand in front (some are detachable and included in the box) and whether the handle is designed to sit flat, increasing its stability and reducing the number of times you'll knock it over. If the gun has no stand, rest it on a ceramic plate or some other fireproof container between shots.

• As you work, the gun will produce ethereal strands of glue that resemble spiderwebs. Just remember to pull them off the project when you're done.

• If you're working with a plastic foam base, test a small area first. Almost all guns will melt foam, but some cause more damage than others. If a deep, moist crater appears on the base, cover it with moss, using floral greening pins. Then glue your materials to the moss.

• Don't hesitate to use as much glue as you need. Many times a small dab will suffice, but some projects conceal globs of glue the size of calamata olives.

• Anything that will melt foam can burn fingers; exercise some care. If you find that you burn yourself frequently, investigate the "warm melt" guns on the market. They use glue sticks that melt at a lower temperature and thus don't get as hot.

• Unplug the gun as soon as you're finished, and never leave an unsupervised child around a gun.

Floral Foam

Foam allows you to convert a pile of flowers into an arrangement and a bag of fruit into a wreath—in other words, the parts into a whole. Since foam isn't nearly as pretty as it is useful, it's at its best covered with greenery or flowers, providing an invisible means of support.

Foam comes in two forms: dry and wet. Each has advantages.

Dry. This is the rigid plastic foam (Styrofoam, for example) readily available in craft shops, discount houses, and department stores. It comes in a variety of shapes—sheets, cones, balls, squares, and rectangles—and is easily cut and shaped even further with a serrated knife.

It also comes in white or green. Given a choice, use whichever color blends best with the materials you're attaching (for example, a green foam base for an herbal wreath). That way, if a section does manage to peek through, it is less glaring.

Some blocks of foam come with a self-adhesive

strip on the bottom, convenient for securing to a container—for example, the bowl that will hold an arrangement. If there's no strip, there's no problem. Floral tape, clay, or wire, a glue gun, or brute force will all work well.

Evergreens and flowers with tough stems can be inserted directly into the foam; just cut the stem at an angle to provide a pointed end. Weak-stemmed flowers must be attached to floral picks and then inserted.

Wet. This fine-grained floral foam (touch it, and a fine dust comes off on your fingers) is invaluable for fresh arrangements. When soaked in water, it will absorb and hold moisture for weeks. Thus, fresh materials inserted into it can absorb moisture as they need it. Wet foam allows you to decorate a tabletop Christmas tree, for example, with fresh carnations that will last through the season.

Wet-type foam comes in "bricks."

Occasionally, designers use dry foam without wetting it, when they're working with especially delicate dried flowers, when they want an especially small piece of foam, or when there's nothing else around the house.

Bases. Even small crafts stores stock a variety of wreath bases: straw, moss, vine, foam, wire, paper, even rattan. In December, foam bases covered with ground cinnamon appear in some craft shops. Sizes range from tiny to huge.

Attachment. Gluing, picking, wiring, pinning—all are legitimate means of getting natural materials to stay where you want them.

Materials. Evergreens, flowers fresh or dried, berries, cones, fruit, nuts, seedheads, pods—if it's pretty enough for you to lean down and pick up, it's wreath material. (Assuming, of course, reasonable size and weight. Fenceposts are probably out.)

Locations. Wreaths have traditionally graced front doors and mantlepieces, but they also look good elsewhere: interior doors, walls, windows, cabinets, and every room of the house, even the bath.

An outside wreath invites your guests inside, whether it's hanging on an exterior wall, a gatepost, a lamppost, or even a tree close to the house.

Tips

All of these suggestions for applying materials are violated regularly and deliberately, with splendid results. But they're still good general rules.

• Start with your background material—something you have lots of, which covers well, and which you like (it will be prominent in the wreath). Possibilities include moss, silver king artemisia, boxwood, bay leaves , and sorghum heads.

• Usually, materials should be inserted into the base at the same angle.

• Framing the outside of the wreath can be effective.

• If the base is attractive, part of it—even most of it—can be left bare. Vine bases are interesting and complex, either natural or misted with paint, and pine needle bases are attractively rough and rustic.

But bare sections need to be deliberate. Unintended bare patches will spoil a wreath. In applying background material, overlap the picked or wired bunches as you go around the wreath, thus covering the base thoroughly.

Making Arrangements

Container. As long as it's stable and will hold a piece of foam large enough to support all the materials you plan to use, the container can be just about anything: vase, flowerpot, pitcher, bowl. Reconnoiter your cupboard. You may find favorite pieces that can be brought out of the closet and used.

Sometimes a container-within-a-container is the solution. Baskets make handsome holders for natural materials, but they're often too large and oddly shaped to fill with foam, always too leaky and easily water-stained to hold fresh flowers. Place a piece of foam in a bowl, the bowl in the basket, and crumpled newspaper around the sides, to hold the bowl in place.

Shape. An arrangement needs an overall shape: triangular, for example, or oval, or round. Whether you make yours vertical or horizonal may depend on where you intend to display it. The overall shape may be defined completely by the materials themselves, or the eye may be allowed to fill in the gaps.

Color. As you look for natural materials, try defining them, not in the usual way, but as colors. You may find that you quite literally see things differently, and stumble upon materials you would otherwise never have thought to use.

Application. Generally, it's useful to establish the boundaries of the arrangement first—to insert the flower or greenery that will provide the highest point, then the materials that will define the outside diameter. With the general shape to guide you, go back and fill in the arrangement.

It's also useful to apply heavy or bulky materials before light, delicate ones. For one thing, the materials are less likely to be damaged that way.

In the arrangement pictured, the designer first inserted the carnations (the highest one first) into the wet foam. With the perimeters drawn, she filled in with bulky galax leaves, then with poms, and, finally, with featherweight spengeri fern.

Focal point. Many arrangements have one component so eye-catching that it inevitably becomes the focal point of the arrangement—all eyes immediately focus on it. If you plan to use a showy bow, for example, or a large, spectacular flower, give some thought to exactly where it should be.

Angle. Consider the height at which the arrangement will be displayed—a high mantlepiece, a low coffee table, a waist-high sideboard—and work on it at that angle. Otherwise, no one may see its best side.

Candles. Metal or plastic candle holders are widely available, ready to insert into the base. Another option is to tape two floral picks to the candle. Not only is a picked candle more stable, but the base takes up less room in the arrangement.

Making Garlands

Perhaps it's all those Victorian woodcuts of merrymakers in long gowns and frock coats, draping greenery down a banister. Whatever the reason, when we plan to deck the halls, we think inevitably of garlands.

Making a garland entails attaching decorative materials to a long "spine"—something thin, flexible, and tough.

If you're dealing with materials that are not conveniently round, you'll need a different spine and a different means of attachment.

Heavy-gauge wire makes a good, durable spine, but the favorite of many designers is jute cord—the type used for macrame. Cut the cord a little longer than you want the garland to be. Some people tie it between two supports—two chair backs, for example—at a comfortable working height; others prefer a work table or the floor.

Wherever you choose to work, form a small bunch of greenery and/or flowers (half a dozen stems or so) and wire the stems together. Then wire the bunch to the spine, using fine, spool-type floral wire. Then wire on another bunch, overlapping the previous one. Continue down the length of the cord, until the garland is finished.

The artistry comes in the composition of the bunches. You can make bunches of individual materials and alternate them down the garland—one bunch of Fraser fir, then one of blue spruce, then gypsophila, then repeat—or each bunch can be composed of several different materials.

After the garland is complete, decorative accents—berries, Christmas balls, knickknacks—can be hot-glued in place. A bow can be wired at either end, at the center, or both.

Making Swags

Broadly defined, swags are bouquets designed to hang—on a wall, a door, a chimney, a cabinet. They can range from beautifully simple to strikingly complex.

Vertical bouquets. The simplest swag consists of greenery or flowers wired together by the stems, usually with a bow wired on to cover the attached stems. Since the design is predictable, all attention focuses on the materials, which need to be very attractive if this decoration is to work.

Horizontal bouquets. Not just bouquets hung by their "ankles," horizonal swags are somewhat more complicated to make (but not much).

Backing. A third type of swag consists of materials attached to a solid backing that gives the decoration shape.

Found objects. Some of the most intriguing swags consist of an object decorated with natural materials. Anything interesting will serve. This is perhaps the most imagination-stretching swag to put together: spotting an everyday object that, with a little dressing up, is worth displaying.

Making Trees

Poet Joyce Kilmer wrote that "only God can make a tree," but then he'd never heard of Styrofoam. If you're trying for only a tabletop model, you have lots of options.

Vine. Vine trees are widely available in craft stores or Christmas shops, ready to be decorated to your taste. Or you can make your own. Gather a good quantity of thin, dried vines—honeysuckle, grapevine, wisteria, whatever grows where you are. (Note: If you're allergic to poison ivy or oak, you will react to the dry vines as you do to the green leaves. It's wise to know what you're getting into.) Another option is to buy a vine wreath and uncurl it.

However you get them, soak the vines for four or five hours, to soften them. Make a cone-shaped cardboard form, and wrap the pliable vines around it. Allow to dry overnight, and remove the tree from its form.

Foam. Plastic foam cones, widely available, supply ready-made tree shapes. They're stable enough to stand upright on their own, and materials can be inserted or picked directly into them, following the basic tree shape. The one shown has boxwood stems inserted into the top and a piece of ground pine picked into the bottom.

A cone can also be glued to the end of an upright tree branch for a Douglas fir shape .

A brick of wet floral foam, stood on end, makes a good base for a tree that includes fresh materials. Tape the foam securely to a shallow container, making the tape bite into the foam, and insert materials so that they form a tree shape. Water the tree from the top, for a long-lasting decoration.

Foam balls are also useful for a topiary style of tree. Hot-glued to the top of a tree branch, they can make an interesting double tree.

Faux tree. (Please. Not "artificial," but "faux." You may be faking it, but you're faking it with class.) A green plastic tree looks undeniably fake, but if it's covered with natural materials, no one will know. Faux trees are so inexpensive and convenient that even the most committed naturalists buy them and hot-glue natural materials onto them.

Plants. Live plants that are naturally tree-shaped—or can be pruned that way—make interesting table trees. A cactus, for example, or a rosemary plant can turn into a Christmas tree overnight.

Making Ornaments

An ornament can be a single interesting item—for example, a milkweed pod—attached to an ornament hanger with a dab of hot glue. It can be a small bunch of berries, dried flowers, or grasses tied with ribbon. It can be a foam or glass ball with natural materials glued onto it.

Walk around your yard, wander through the woods, and scan the roadsides as you drive, redefining what you see. Is that a Christmas ornament that no one else has recognized?

Then head for the crafts store, scanning not just the Christmas section but other areas as well. Small baskets offer endless possibilities, as do other miniature containers (flowerpots, toy watering cans, wheelbarrows, kitchen implements). The dried materials are worth considering: a lotus pod makes an interesting ornament.

Tips

• Think light. An ornament doesn't have to be very heavy at all to make a fir branch as droopy as the post-Christmas blues.

• Keep in mind that the ornament will be displayed on a green tree. Unless the observer is very close indeed, or the texture is markedly different, greenery on an ornament won't show up.

• Be sure to attach the hanger (whether ribbon or wire) so that the ornament will hang with the correct side out. Since tree branches usually project out from the center of the tree, most hangers should go from side to side, rather than from front to back.

• An excellent hanger for foam balls is a "hairpin" made of heavy-gauge floral wire, stuck into the ball. A commercial wire hanger can attach to that.

Decorating Packages

A present that is hand-decorated with natural materials sends a special warmth. It makes a gift, not only of the contents, but of your time and creativity as well.

To create distinctive packages, you'll need only natural materials and a glue gun. After wrapping the package with paper in the normal fashion, position the materials in a pleasing arrangement, and hot-glue them to the paper or to each other. If desired, add a bow or mix in some artificial fruit, berries, or a small bird.

Tips

• Consider the package as a whole: the paper, the natural materials, and (if you're using one) the ribbon. Make sure the colors of paper and the naturals complement each other.

• When selecting natural materials, try for a variety of shapes and textures. On the package below, fuzzy strawflowers and rigid pine cones provide contrasting textures.

• Arrange the natural materials in an identifiable shape—a crescent, circle, or rectangle, for example.

It helps to do a few dry runs, laying out the materials in a variety of combinations on a scrap of paper before actually gluing them down.

• Start with relatively flat background materials, then add the more three-dimensional items.

• Packages can be wrapped in fabric, rather than paper, with natural materials hot-glued on in the same fashion—often with memorable results.

Making Corn Husk Flowers

Corn husks can be purchased at craft stores or shucked from actual ears of corn. If you peel your own, be careful not to tear the husks as you remove them; the larger the husks, the easier they are to work with. Spread them in the sun to dry, keeping them in a thin layer and turning them often, so they'll dry quickly without mildew.

If you want colored flowers, fabric dyes work well on corn husks. Dissolve approximately half a package of dye in half a gallon of water, and heat to boiling. (Actual amounts can vary with the stiffness of the husks and the amount of natural yellow they have.) Dip the husks in the hot dye. If you want a deep hue, remove the dye from the heat and let the husks soak overnight.

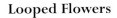

Looped Flowers

1. Tear your stiffest husks lengthwise into strips. You'll need five strips about 1-3/4 inches (4.4 cm.) wide for the petals.

2. Use your less attractive husks to make the center. Roll the husks into a roll about 3/4 inch in diameter, and wire with firm wire about an inch (2.5 cm.) from the top. Trim the wire ends and excess corn husk, leaving about an inch of husk below the wire.

3. Fold the petal strips in half and position them around the center. Wire them to the center either one by one or all at once, whichever is easier.

4. Trim excess husks from the bottom, tapering the base instead of cutting straight across.

5. Cut a piece of heavy wire about 18 inches (45 cm.) long. Make a "fish hook" in one end and insert the other end into the center. Carefully pull the wire down through the flower until the hook anchors in the center. Tape the flower to the wire with masking tape, covering the flower's tapered base and about 1/2 inch (1.25 cm.) of the wire. Wrap the base and the entire stem with floral tape.

Shaggy Flowers

1. Gather pieces of husk in a bundle, with the natural points in the same direction. The fatter the bundle, the larger the flower. A good working diameter is two inches (5 cm.).

2. Wire the bundle tightly with heavy floral wire about 5-1/2 inches (13.75 cm.) from the top (the pointed ends), and trim off excess husk, tapering the cut.

3. Tear the husks into large strips. Or shred the husks with a hat pin, for a wispy, curly effect. Shredded husks will curl naturally as they continue to dry.

4. Add a stem as described for the looped flowers. The stem can remain beautifully long and straight,

for arrangements, or twist around a wreath base for anchoring.

Making Bows

To have tried to make a bow is to understand despair. The ribbon seems to take on a life (and a passive-aggressive personality) of its own, wriggling out of your fingers one moment, lying there limply the next. And it's small comfort that every smart-aleck you talk to says there's nothing to it.

There's nothing to it. Especially at Christmas, craft stores stock ready-made, red velvet bows in various sizes and will probably make you a bow of any ribbon in stock.

On the other hand, there are wonderful ribbons—watered silk, paper, raffia, taffeta, grosgrain, metallic, net, lace, velvet cord, satin tapestry—sold by places that do not make bows. If you do, you can turn a good project into a smashing one.

Picked Loops

An easy option is to wire loops of ribbon onto floral picks. Just fold a piece of ribbon loosely in half, pinch the ends together against a pick, and wrap the wire around the ribbon. The picked loops at the lower left of this page were made three different ways: with a tail, with two loops, and with a single loop. To create a bow, pick the loops into the base of your project, one on top of the other.

Real Bows

1. Form a circle at the end of the ribbon. (The one in the photo is lying on its side.)

2. Pinch the circle together in the center, and hold it there. This is even easier than it sounds.

3. Adding to the back of the bow, form loops of ribbon, first on one side, then the other, continuing until the bow is as full as you want it. This is harder than it sounds.

4. Wire the bow together in the center, leaving long enough wire ends for attaching to the project.

5. Shape the bow, pulling the loops into position. Move a loop around by inserting your finger inside it and pulling; if you pinch the loop closed, it will flatten.

Tips

• The key words are "pinch and twist." As you complete each new loop by bringing the ribbon back to the center of the bow, pinch the ribbon in the middle and twist it, so that the upper side becomes the lower one. Otherwise, half of the loops will be wrong-side-out.

• A bow wired onto a pick is often easier to insert in an arrangement or wreath.

• Don't underestimate the amount of ribbon you'll need. A decent-sized bow can eat up four yards of ribbon without even trying.

• Learning to make bows is largely a matter of fiddling with a ribbon until until you like the result, then repeating the process until you've got it down.

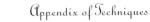
GENERAL TOLE PAINTING INSTRUCTIONS

Supplies You Will Need

To Have on Hand:

Acrylic Paints

Brush Basin

Chalk Pencil or
   Soapstone Pencil

Cloths

Flow Medium

Glazing Medium

Hot-Glue Gun

Liquid Soap

Metal Primer

Mop

Paintbrushes

Paper Towels

Pencils

Polyurethane

Water-Based Varnish

Retarder or Extender

Rubbing Alcohol

Sandpaper

Sponges

Spray Varnish

Stylus

Tack Cloth

Tracing Paper

Transfer Paper or
   Graphite Paper

Transparent Tape

Vinegar

Waxed Palette

Wood Glue

Wood Putty

Wood Sealer

Paintbrushes:

Almost any brand of paintbrush is good when it is new. The most important thing is that it needs to be clean and well shaped. When paint begins to build up inside the ferrule, the paintbrush will no longer perform the way it was intended.

For most acrylic painting, synthetic paintbrushes are best, but there are certain techniques where a natural-bristled paintbrush is more suitable.

A paintbrush should have enough "snap" to it to return to its original shape after painting a stroke. Paintbrushes that are too soft and lack body make painting difficult. Your greatest investment as a painter will be in quality paintbrushes. You will need a variety of styles and sizes. A good set of brushes should include, but not be limited to:

Sizes 4, 8, 12, 14 Flats

Sizes 2, 4 Liners

Sizes 0, 2, 4 Rounds

0, 1, 10/0 Script Liners

Sizes 4, 6, 8 Filberts

Sizes 3/4", 1" Flat Wash(s)

Sizes 3/4", 1/2" Rakes (Tooth)

Size 3 Quill (Raphael Kolinsky®)

In addition, there are a number of "specialty" paintbrushes available that have specific purposes. These may include a Rake (Tooth or Comb), Fan, Deerfoot, and Dagger. It is good to have a supply of old worn-out paintbrushes on hand also.

Paintbrush Care:

Most commercial brush basins were designed with at least three compartments. One or two for cleaning—they have teeth on the bottom for gently forcing the paint out of the paintbrush. The other compartment is for rinsing.

If you will always wash and rinse your paintbrush before you set it down, you will be able to walk away from your painting at any time and know that your paintbrushes are not being ruined by dry paint.

Every so often it is a good idea to give your paintbrushes a bit of extra care. Clean them with liquid soap, pinch out excess water, and let them air dry. It is best to let them dry lying down so that water does not soak into the handle through the ferrule. Once dry, it is recommended that paintbrushes be stored upright in a container.

Rubbing alcohol can remove paint from a totally neglected paintbrush, but it cannot restore its shape. Once a paintbrush loses its chisel or point, do yourself a favor and get a new brush—you will be glad you did!

Wood Preparation:

The majority of the projects in this book are painted on wooden surfaces. Check for holes, cracks, and other imperfections in the surface.

If necessary, fill with wood putty. In any case, sand until smooth. Wipe with a tack cloth to remove dust. Apply one coat of wood sealer, following manufacturer's directions, and let dry. Don't neglect to seal your wood, as it will make a big difference in your painting. Floating, linework, and strokework will be much easier to do if you have properly prepared your painting surface. When the sealer is dry, lightly sand with a superfine sandpaper. Again wipe with a tack cloth to remove dust. Remember—sand, seal, sand.

Galvanized Metal

Preparation:

Galvanized metal has an oily film that must be removed before painting. Using a moistened cloth, wash the metal surface with a mixture of vinegar and water (1:1), but do not immerse the piece in water. To roughen the surface, lightly sand with a superfine sandpaper. Wipe with a tack cloth to remove dust. Spray the piece with several light coats of metal primer, following manufacturer's directions, and let dry for 24 hours before proceeding.

Transferring Patterns:

Begin by tracing or copying your design onto a piece of tracing paper—something that you can see through. Sometimes this can be a bit tedious, but it is important to be able to see through your paper so that you can accurately place it on your painting surface. Tracing will also help familiarize you with the design before you begin to paint.

After placing the pattern over the surface, slide a piece of transfer or graphite paper between the design and the surface. Using a stylus, trace the design again. Transfer only the main elements of the design—do not transfer details that will be covered up by base-coating.

Sometimes pieces are oddly shaped and sculpted. Applying a traced pattern with transfer or graphite paper is nearly impossible and is rarely done accurately. The best way to apply a guide for painting is to draw it.

You are now ready to begin painting. Following is a list of painting terms along with a brief description of each for your reference.

Working with Acrylic Paints:

Begin by squeezing a "puddle" of paint about the size of a nickel onto your palette. Using a paintbrush, pull the paint from the edge of the puddle. Avoid dipping the paintbrush in the center of the puddle.

Let each coat of paint dry before applying another coat.

Base-Coating:

Base-coating is simply covering an entire area with one initial color of acrylic paint until the surface is opaque. Paint must be smooth, without ridges or brush strokes. Starting in the center and painting toward the outer edges will prevent ridges on the edges. Light coats are better than heavy coats. For better coverage, apply several light coats as necessary.

Floating:

Floating, or side-loading, is an imperative technique to master in order to create soft shadows and highlights. Ninety-nine percent of the time you should float with a size 12 or larger flat paintbrush. Even tiny eyes can be floated with a large brush if it is loaded correctly.

Most of the shading and highlighting on the projects in this book are done with floating. The paintbrush is dipped in clean water, then blotted on a paper towel until the "shine" disappears. Be careful not to remove all the water from the bristles as there is a certain amount of water needed in order to create a softly blended stroke. Dip the corner of the paintbrush into some fresh paint. Begin blending both sides of the paintbrush on your palette. When properly blended, the paintbrush should have paint on one side and clean water on the other. Paint should never reach the water side of the paintbrush. If it does, rinse the paintbrush and start over.

Whenever possible, begin the floating strokes away from you and draw it toward you instead of painting sideways or backhanded. Set the flat surface of the paintbrush down and give it some pressure—you want to "squeeze" the paint and water out of the paintbrush as you apply the stroke. Practice on mat board or cardboard that has been based with several coats of acrylic paint. Do not use paper as paper soaks the water out of the brush and makes floating impossible. Several strokes, such as "S" strokes and "C" strokes, are created with floating. These strokes simply resemble the appropriate letters.

Washing:

Applying a wash onto a surface will allow a very thin, transparent coat of paint to cover the surface. When washing, create a mixture of up to 80% water to 20% paint. It is especially important to let each application dry before applying subsequent layers.

Dry-Brushing:

Dry-brushing is used for adding shading and highlighting to certain areas of a design. Load a dry paintbrush with an appropriate value of paint, then wipe most of the paint from the paintbrush onto a dry paper towel. Dry-brush onto the surface by gently "scrubbing" the area. Be patient and let the color build up gradually.

When dry-brushing cheeks, remove all of the paint from the paintbrush, leaving only a small amount of pigment in the bristles. Gently "scrub" in a circular motion until you achieve the desired brightness.

You can dry-brush small, thin areas such as

stems and vines with a small liner brush. The paint does not need to be as dry as in the previous method, but the paintbrush should not be overloaded. Wipe some of the paint out of the paintbrush before applying it to the surface. Stroke the paint repeatedly in the small areas, "coaxing" the paint from the paintbrush.

Stippling:

Stippling is used to render a textured look to a specific element of a design such as fur, trees, and grass. It is done by "pouncing" with an up-and-down motion on the surface with a paintbrush specifically designed for this purpose, or with an old worn-out paintbrush that no longer holds a chisel edge.

Depending on the effect desired, stippling can be done with a heavy application of paint or with a light application of paint.

Double-Loading:

Using an appropriately sized flat paintbrush for the project you are painting, fully load the paintbrush in the medium value of paint, then pick up a small amount of the light or dark value on the corner of the paintbrush. Blend both sides of the brush on your palette, blending the colors together to create two values on the same paintbrush. Blending is very important, allowing a transition in value—you do not want a sharp line in the center.

Reverse Teardrops:

Reverse teardrops are a traditional stroke used extensively in rosemaling, but they are also used in other forms of folk art. The best paintbrush that I have found for perfecting these strokes is the Raphael Kolinsky® Quill #3.

Load the paintbrush with fresh paint. Holding the paintbrush with the handle upward, lightly set the tip of the paintbrush down and begin to drag as you increase pressure on the paintbrush. End the stroke by setting the belly of the paintbrush down, creating the fat, rounded end of the stroke. Lift the brush straight up.

Double-loaded reverse teardrops are executed in the same way; however, they have two values of paint in the paintbrush. Load the paintbrush in the light value, then tip in the dark value.

Linework:

Linework can make or ruin a beautiful painting project. Learning to do nice linework takes practice, but is well worth the effort.

Linework is best done with a long-bristled paintbrush—a scroller or script liner. Paint should be slightly thinner than when it comes from the bottle. Flow Medium or water can be added, but the end result should be an "inky" con-

sistency. Load the paintbrush, then drag it through the paint and roll the tip into a fine point. Hold your paintbrush handle upward, dragging it along the pattern line. If necessary, use your little finger as a brace.

Finishing:

There are a number of ways to finish a project. For special heirloom pieces, items that are intended for use, or pieces that may get handled repeatedly, it is recommended that from three or four coats to as many as ten coats of polyurethane water-based varnish, matte or satin, be applied.

When using a spray varnish, make certain to remove all pattern lines before varnishing. Also remember to varnish your project before gluing on embellishments such as hair, clothing, and other accessories.

Index

A

Alaimo, Tenley Rae, 132
Amaretto, 162
Andersen, Hans Christian, 168-169
Angels, 50
"Angels We Have Heard on High," 144
Apple juice, 109, 110
Arrangements, 49, 67, 119, 152, 156, 211-212
Ascik, Elizabeth, 196
Avonlea Inn, 68-73
"Away in a Manger," 10

B

Baby breath, 90
Balls, glass, 65-66
Baltimore Eggnog, 109
Bena, Bill, 190
Beverages, 34, 80, 109-110, 138, 161-162
Boots, 127
Bourbon, 138
Bows, 215-216
Brandy, 80, 109
Brothers Grimm, 170-171
Buttered Applejack, 109

C

Calendula, 130
Calvados, 110
Canadian Cocoa, 161
Candlelit Cottage, 74-75
Candles, 56-57, 152, 212
    tints, 84

Candy, 33-34, 93, 183, 200
Candy Land Christmas, 183
Capps family, 103
Carols, 11-13, 36-41, 140, 141, 142-143, 144, 164, 165
Cathedral at Christmas, 160
Centerpieces, 49, 119, 152, 211-212
Cheese, 104-105
Cherubs, 48, 50
Chili Pepper Wreath, 115
Chocolate, 206-207
Christmas Cheer, 80
Christmas cherries, 130
Christmas Tree Santa, 28-29
Christmas Wedding Chapel, 159
Cider, 109
Ciderific, 109
Cinnamon, 109
    oil, 84
Cinnamon Warmer, 110
Classic Gingerbread House, 32-33
Cocoa, 110, 161
Coffee, 161, 162
Color flow, 74, 200-201
"Come, O Come, Emmanuel," 40
Cook, Kristen, 68-73, 191, 206
Copper Ribbon Wreath, 49
Corn Husk and Straw Wreath, 117
Cotton bolls, 116, 131
Cotton Seed Ornaments, 131
Cotton Seed Wraps, 114
Cotton Wreath, 116
Coventry Alley, 76-79
Covered Bridge Mill, 100-101
Cowboy Santa ornaments, 122-123, 126

Crème de cacao, 161
Crème de menthe, 110

D

"Deck the Halls," 36
Decorations, 55, 82, 146-148
    See also Arrangements; Centerpieces; Ornaments, tree.
Delaplane, Stanton, 161
Dill, 107
Dioramas, 30-32
Dried Pepper Ornaments, 129-130

E

Editorials, 166-167
Eggnog, 34, 80, 109, 138
Eggs, 30-31
"The Elves and the Shoemaker," 170-171
Evergreen Swag, 27

F

Feliz Navidad, 158
Fir, 89, 156
Fir Tree Topiary, 156
Fire starters, 83-84
"The First Noel," 141
Floral foam, 210
Flower Topiary, 67
Flowers, 211-212
    corn husk, 214-215
    crepe paper, 99
Foam cones, 213
Fondant, 132, 206, 209
Fraser Fir Wreath, 89
Fredrickson, Sally, 33, 192, 201

G

Gadberry, Vicki, 112
Garlands, 122-123, 212
Gift bags, 42, 92
"The Gift of the Magi," 16-20
Gift wrapping, 42-45, 114, 214
Gingerbread, 71, 72, 73, 185-209
Gingerbread houses, 32-33, 68-73,
        74-75, 76-79, 93, 100-101,
        102, 103, 132-133, 134, 157,
        158, 159, 160, 182, 183, 184
    baking and building, 185-209
    construction tips, 190, 191, 192,
        196, 197, 200, 201, 204, 208,
        209
    doors, 197
    edibility, 197
    lighting, 207
    roofs, 196, 197
    trimmings, 192, 196-209
    windows, 197, 198, 200
Glass Ball Ornaments, 65-66
Glitter, 97, 181
Glue, 181, 210
Glue guns, 210
Glühwein, 162
Goelz, Lisa, 159
Gourds, 176-177
Graham crackers, 93, 158
Grand Marnier, 80, 110
Grant, President Ulysses S., 138
Greenery Wreath with Ribbon, 88
Gruber, Franz, 140

H

Handermann, David, 204
"Happy New Year" (phrase), 145
"Hark, the Herald Angels Sing," 38
Henry, O., 16-20
Hensley, Christi, 153
Herbed Cheese, 104-105
Herbs, 104-105, 115
Holiday Village, 157
"The Holly and the Ivy," 39
Hot Buttered Rum, 34
Hot chocolate. See Cocoa.
Hot Eggnog, 80

Hot Glue and Glitter Wreath, 181
Hot Scotch Toddy, 161

I

Icing, royal, 101, 103, 132, 158, 192,
        201, 202, 204, 208, 209
Interior decoration, 92-99, 118-127,
        50-55
Irish Coffee, 161
Irwin, Dana, 28
Italian Coffee, 162

J

Jerked Spice Blend, 135
Jingle Bell Sleigh, 172-175
Jingle Bells, 164
Johnson, Pam, 134
"Jolly Old St. Nicholas," 12
"Joy to the World," 165
Jute cord, 123, 213

K

Kitchens, 97

L

Licorice, 132-133, 183
Linens, 50-51
"The Little Match-Seller," 168-169
Lollipops, 183, 204

M

Madeira, 109
Mangers, 25-26
Marzipan, 205, 208, 209
McCallister, Trish, 74, 157
"Merry Christmas" (phrase) 145
Merry-Go Round, 184
Midnight Snowstorm, 110
Mohr, Joseph, 140
Moore, Clement Clarke, 14-15
Mountain Hideaway, 102
Mulled Wine, 80

N

Nativities, 25-27
Necco wafers, 196
Needlepoint, 146-148

Needlepoint Ornaments, 146-148
New York Sun, 166

O

"O Come All Ye Faithful," 37
O'Hanlon, Virginia, 166
Ornaments, Christmas tree, 28-29,
        30-31, 54-55, 58-62, 63-64,
        65-66, 99, 122-123, 126, 129-130,
        131, 146-148, 213-214

P

Packages, 42-45, 114, 214
Painted Egg Ornaments, 30-31
Papier-maché, 46, 153-155
Paraffin, 84
Pastillage, 205, 209
Paté, 106
Peppers, 115, 129-130
Phrases, multi-lingual, 145
Pierpont, James, 164
Pillows, 50-51, 112-113
Pine, 21, 47, 90
Pine and Baby Breath Swag, 90
Pine, Fruit and Gold Wreath, 47
Pine Wreath, 21
Pinecone Fire Starters, 83-84
Place mats, 85-86, 97
Place Mats with Decorative Stitching,
        85-86
Planters, 94
Poems, 14-15
Poinsettias, 96-97
Portraits, 94
Potpourri, 66
Pretzels, 202
Prints, 94
Prism Ornaments, 63-64
Puppets, 176-177

Q

Quilting, 85-86

R

Ramsey, Alan, 161
Recipes, 104-105, 106-107, 108, 135,
        136, 137, 208-209

See also Beverages.
Red and Green Salsas, 136-137
Reurs, Catherine, 146
Ribbon, 215-216
Rolled Beeswax Candles, 56-57
Ropin' Cowboy Kringle, 123
Ruby, Mary Beth, 46
Rum, 34, 80, 109, 110, 138, 161
Russell, Alex, 77, 79

S

Salmon, 106
Salsa, 136, 137
Salsa Roja, 136
Salsa Verde, 137
Samplers, 149-151
Santa Claus, 23, 28-29, 46, 112, 122,
    123, 126, 146-148, 149-151,
    153-155, 166-167, 176-177,
    178-180
Santa Hand Puppet, 176-177
Santa Star Pillow, 112-113
Santa Wreath, 23
Santa's Palace, 182
Santa's Sampler, 149-151
Sayings, multi-lingual, 145
Scheible, Pat, 10
Searcy, Judy, 190
Sheridan, Joe, 161
Silent Night, 140
Sleds. *See* Sleighs.
Sleighs, 82, 94-95, 172-175
Smith, June, 197

Smith, Shannon, 197
Smoked Trout Paté, 106
Snack Basket, 108
Snow Bunny, 110
Snow-Covered Cottage, 103
Somersaulting Santa, 178-180
Stories, 16-20, 168-169, 170-171
Summit, Ginger, 176
Swags, 24, 90, 122-123, 128, 213

T

Table Wreath with Candles, 152
Thomas, Jerry, 138
Tissue boxes, 124-125
Tod's Well, 161
Toddies, 161, 162
Tole-Painted Nativity, 25-26
Tole painting, 25-27, 217-220
Tootsie rolls, 202
Topiaries, 67, 156
Tote bags. *See* Gift bags.
Totem Pole Lodge, 132-133
Toys, 178-180
Traditional Berry Wreath, 22
Traditional Log House, 134
Trays, 50
Trees, 67, 213
Trout, 106-107
Trunks, 12
The Twelve Days of Christmas, 142-143

U

Up on the Housetop, 13

V

Vacation Eggnog, 138
Victorian Father Christmas, 46
Victorian Ornaments, 58-62
Victorian Wraps, 42-45
Vines, 213-214
Violin and Cherub Wreath, 48
A Visit from St. Nicholas, 14-15

W

We Three Kings, 11
We Wish You a Merry Christmas, 41
Wheat, 128
Wheat Swags, 128
Wheelbarrows, 94
Whiskey, 138, 161
White Pine Wreath, 87
Wine, 80, 109, 162
Wondrous Santa, 153-155
Wreathes, 21-23, 47, 48, 49, 87, 88,
    89, 91, 94, 115, 116, 117, 118,
    152, 181, 211

Y

Yes, Virginia, There is a Santa Claus,
    166-167
Young, Emily Grace, 158